The Extraordinary Story of Mary Eames

Paddy Butler

About the Author

Paddy Butler is a journalist of long standing and a former foreign correspondent working from Paris and London. During a career which began in the *Irish Press* he has worked as a freelance journalist in Paris, a freelance sub-editor for the *Times* of London and a staff journalist for the *Financial Times*. In Paris he worked on Radio France International's English service, where he co-hosted a nightly live broadcast to Africa. In 2012 he broke the remarkable – and hitherto unknown – story of Mary Elmes in the *Irish Times*. He followed this up in the same publication in 2013 with the story of her being honoured as Righteous Among the Nations. He is also an executive producer of Midas Productions' documentary on Mary Elmes, *It Tolls for Thee*.

If you have any further information on Mary Elmes and the children she saved during the Second World War please contact him on maryelmesbook@gmail.com.

THE EXTRAORDINARY STORY OF MARY ELMES

The Irish Oskar Schindler

Paddy Butler

ORPEN PRESS

Published by
Orpen Press
Upper Floor, Unit K9
Greenogue Business Park
Rathcoole
Co. Dublin
Ireland

email: info@orpenpress.com
www.orpenpress.com

Photographs are reproduced with the kind permission of Caroline and Patrick Danjou, Ron Friend, the American Friends Service Committee and the author.

Paperback ISBN 978-1-78605-044-1
ePub ISBN 978-1-78605-045-8

A catalogue record for this book is available from the British Library.

Printed in Dublin by SPRINTprint Ltd

For Vivienne

In memory of Andreas Freund (1925–1996), a dear friend and mentor

Acknowledgements

In the years since I first began researching the story of Mary Elmes many people around the world have helped me along the way towards publishing this book. I wish to express my gratitude, first and foremost, to my wife and soulmate, Vivienne McBride, without whose unfailing patience, constant support and wise counsel this book would never have appeared. Special thanks also go to Bernard Wilson, who willingly shared with me his own vast knowledge of Mary's life and has provided constant back-up support throughout this project. My grateful thanks are also due to Donald Davis, archivist at the AFSC, who granted me permission to access that organisation's files and subsequently provided clear and prompt answers to my many queries. Andrew Gallimore, director of the documentary on Mary's life – *It Tolls for Thee* – has been an inspirational colleague and friend, whose acute insights and sound advice have proved invaluable to me while writing this book. I would also like to thank Mary's son and daughter, Patrick and Caroline Danjou, for my warm welcome into their family and the wealth of information they provided through their own collections of material pertaining to their mother's life. Special thanks also go to Mark Elmes, Mary's cousin in Cork, for his kind support and hospitality. Grateful thanks are due to Ron Friend, not only for sharing his life story with me, but also for his advice and support.

I wish to thank Mark Derby for allowing me to quote from his book *Petals and Bullets*; likewise Linda Pelfreeman (*Aristocrats, Adventurers and Ambulances*) and Rosemary Bailey, whose book *Love and War in the Pyrenees* played a pivotal role in taking the story of Mary Elmes to a wider audience. I am grateful to my editors at Orpen Press, Ailbhe O'Reilly and Eileen O'Brien, for their skill and support.

Thanks are also due, in no particular order, to Mack Morun, John Morgan, Rose Duroux, Roger Barrié, Mimi Leder, Stephen Harte, Patsy McGarry, Marcela Arteaga, Mike Keane at Midas Productions, the family of Sir George and Lady Young, the Irish Department of Foreign Affairs and the United States Holocaust Memorial Museum.

For their unfailing ability to provide out-of-hours technical computer support a special 'thank you' goes to Nathalia Tysiak, Lilly Whelan and Primo Sese.

Contents

Prologue

Perpignan, Occupied France
February 1943

In her first-floor apartment on the Avenue des Baléares, behind a door she keeps permanently double-locked, an Irishwoman in her mid-thirties is poring over a series of counterfeit documents. She sits straight-backed at her desk, the forgeries laid out before her in rows, as neatly as a fortune-teller's cards. Despite the privations wrought by wartime rationing she is, as always, immaculately dressed; her fair, shoulder-length hair is neatly pinned up at the back of her neck, her blouse freshly ironed. She scrutinises each document for the tiniest flaw, vaguely aware of the icy Tramontane wind outside, sweeping down from the desolate peaks of the Pyrenees to rattle her windows and rustle the geraniums on the balcony. A fireplace is tucked into the wall opposite her desk but in this time of war and occupation French coal fuels the Nazi war machine and the mound of ashes in the hearth has lain cold and grey for weeks.

It is early afternoon. Outside, a few passers-by foraging for whatever they can find on the black market wander beneath the bare plane trees.

An official-looking black car suddenly lurches on to the avenue, its two stoney-faced occupants smugly noting the palpable unease their arrival provokes among those watching. Outside Number 30 the car glides to a halt. The driver ducks out on to the pavement, straightens up in his well-cut overcoat and dons a black fedora, mentally noting the comforting weight of the Luger pistol in his right-hand pocket. His companion is dressed as though they are twins. The sight of the men's clothes, instantly recognisable as the preferred civilian garb of Nazi Gestapo officers, transforms the mood among those watching from apprehension to dread.

The woman they are here to take has been shadowed for some time by French Intelligence officers. The Gestapo men have seen her dossier. They have read how she ran hospitals for children in Spain during the Spanish Civil War before making her way to France. They also know that she uses her current role as an aid worker in the nearby Rivesaltes transit camp as a cover to help Jews escape deportation, that she supplies enemies of the Reich with false identity papers and exit visas, and hides these people where they can't be found. She has even been seen placing children in the boot of her car before brazenly driving them past the camp guards.

The men are at the main door of her building.

One floor above them, the Irishwoman calmly goes about her work. And yet – as she would confide to her family decades later – sitting at her desk on this wintry day she is suddenly gripped by a premonition of imminent catastrophe. A persistent, shrill ring reverberates through the building. She listens for the habitual creak of the concierge crossing the hall and bristles at the unfamiliar murmur of low, dark voices below.

She is on her feet now, snatching up the forgeries as she runs to her hiding place in the bathroom, swiftly stooping to slide the documents under the linoleum beneath the bath.

The men are throwing their weight against her door, shouting out her name. She steadies herself and calls out in response, surveying the apartment one final time before unlocking the door. Once inside, the men flash Gestapo identification cards and inform her that she is under arrest.

She watches as the pair ransack the apartment, emptying drawers onto the floor, sweeping her books from their shelves, flinging her clothes and bedding on to the parquet in a fruitless search for evidence against her.

The Irishwoman confronts the one she assumes is the senior of the two, protests that she is a citizen of a neutral country and a bona fide aid worker accredited to a Quaker humanitarian organisation. His reply is to bundle her towards the door. Outside on the avenue some of those defiantly lingering recognise their neighbour, taller than the men flanking her, being hustled into their car and driven away.

***

Seventy-one years later, on a sun-filled June day, before a jubilant audience in a crowded municipal hall in southwest France, her family accept on her behalf Israel's highest honour to non-Jews who risked their lives to save Jewish people during the Holocaust. Unacknowledged in life, she is posthumously recognised as Righteous Among the Nations, the only Irish person to be so named.

During her long lifetime she herself never sought recognition for the risks she ran or the lives she saved in Spain and France – even spurning the offer of France's highest honour, the Légion d'Honneur. But a two-year-old boy she rescued with his older brother from the industrialised killing machine that murdered their father ensured decades later that their saviour was credited for giving so many others the gift of life by placing in peril her own.

Her name was Mary Elmes. This is her story.

1

The Caravan of Death

Miguel Escalona Quesada was just ten years old when he and a group of fellow orphans were hastily put aboard a bus on the southern coast of a Spain convulsed by civil war. It was early February 1937, six months after a fascist army coup against the fledgling democratic government sparked the conflict, and for the city of Malaga, until now a bastion of radical, Republican resistance in the south, time was running out. Rebel forces led by Genera Queipo de Llano – a bloodthirsty, vain loudmouth – were tightening their grip on the city and closing in for a deadly finale.

Queipo de Llano, or the Butcher of Andalusia as he would become known, was in command of a large mixed force of men, including Italian 'Blackshirt' units provided by fellow fascist Benito Mussolini, backed by tanks and armoured vehicles. His Nationalist Army of the South also included 10,000 battle-hardened colonial Moroccan 'Moorish' troops, whose reputation for barbarity was such that the mere sight of their distinctive white turbans provoked terror among those caught in their path.

Nationalist rebel gains elsewhere in the country had effectively cut off Malaga from the rest of Republican Spain. Moreover, its defenders – mainly comprising ill-trained and badly armed trades union militias under the control of bickering anarchist or socialist parties – were no match for the forces closing in on the city and its panic-stricken inhabitants.

In a desperate attempt to out-run the imminent fall of the city, the orphans joined more than 120,000 desperate refugees fleeing to Almeria, further east along the coast. As the children were boarding their bus a military aircraft swooped out of nowhere, spraying machine-gun fire and bombs. "Many ran away, whilst others stayed on the bus so as not to lose their seat to Almeria", Miguel recalled. "We came back and found our luggage and the buses burning; those who had stayed were dead and out of eighty children at the orphanage ten of us were left … on our own."

On February 6, with Queipo de Llano's troops in control of the high ground overlooking the city, Malaga's Republican commander, Colonel Villalba, had ordered the city's evacuation, triggering the flight of more than 120,000 of its inhabitants along the only escape route left open to them – the 109-mile coastal road to Almeria. Refugees already fleeing Queipo de Llano's trail of carnage through Andalusia swelled the human flood struggling along the coastal road, framed by the sea on one side and the Sierra Nevada mountain range on the other. Without military protection the terrified thongs were defenceless against the onslaught.

"Start digging graves", Queipo de Llano had repeatedly warned in his nightly propaganda radio broadcasts. It was to prove no idle boast.

In biting winter cold the desperate fugitives had set off for Almeria – a pitiful crush of mainly women and children, the elderly and the infirm, whose menfolk were still fighting at the frontlines of the war. Weighed down by cloth bundles or suitcases containing a few hastily gathered possessions, most of the refugees travelled on foot, although a fortunate few rode donkeys. For most, the nightmare journey would take five days and nights.

Running Queipo de Llano's gauntlet left the refugees prey to relentless attacks. By the time the first of those fleeing reached Motril, halfway to Almeria, he gleefully announced, "To accompany them in their flight and make them run more quickly, we sent our aviation to bomb them." The attacks were unrelenting and came from all sides: in addition to the air raids, warships prowling offshore lobbed shell after shell at the refugees on a road frequently made impassable by stalled vehicles and the dead and dying littering the road. Those who lagged behind were mercilessly sprayed with machine-gun fire by their Italian pursuers. At night the lights of the Italian armoured vehicles flickered in the distance like spectres, compounding the terror of the refugees stumbling along the darkened road. In the chaos, children whose parents lay dead beside them were left to fend for themselves.

Canadian doctor Norman Bethune, who had brought a mobile blood transfusion unit to Spain, operated a shuttle service for the refugees with his lorry. For three days and nights, Bethune, his assistant, Hazen Size, and driver, T.C. Worsley, ferried people to Almeria. Worsley's account paints a stark picture of the nightmare scenes they witnessed:

> The refugees still filled the road and the further we got the worse was their condition. A few of them were wearing rubber shoes, but most feet were bound with rags, many feet were bare, nearly all were bleeding. There were seventy miles of people desperate with hunger and exhaustion and still the streams showed no sign of diminishing. … We decided to fill the lorry with kids. Instantly we were the centre of a mob of raving, shouting people, entreating and begging, at this sudden miraculous apparition. The scene was fantastic, of the shouting faces of the women holding up naked babies above their heads, pleading, crying and sobbing with gratitude or disappointment.

As historian Paul Preston points out, "The reports of numerous eyewitnesses, including Lawrence Fernsworth, the correspondent of *The Times*, made it impossible for rebel supporters to deny one of the most horrendous atrocities perpetrated against Republican civilians."

In Malaga those who had been unable to flee were shown no mercy when Queipo de Llano's forces swept into the beleaguered city. Preston has described how, despite the ease of victory and lack of resistance, "Civilians were not allowed to enter the city for a week while hundreds of Republicans were shot on the basis of denunciations. In the seven weeks following the capture of Malaga, 3,401 people were tried on the basis of 'urgent summary courts martial', of whom 1,574 were executed."

Despite their brush with death, the plucky Miguel and the other survivors of the bus attack pressed on alone on foot towards Almeria.

"We were really hungry, we walked bare-foot and at night we slept huddled together because it was cold and damp." One image that carved itself into his memory was that of a woman injured by a howitzer shell, lying in a pool of blood, struggling to breastfeed her infant child. Miraculously, Miguel and his companions made it to Almeria and from there to France, where he had relatives. After the war he returned to Spain and worked in the family business before becoming involved in local politics. When Torremolinos became independent of Malaga he was elected mayor of the city in 1988 and re-elected in 1991. He died in 2011.

***

While this humanitarian crisis was unfolding along the Spanish coast, a gifted young Irishwoman working in London was invited to embark on an extraordinary mission to the centre of the conflict by an eccentric former diplomat called Sir George Young. Sir George, then 65 years old, was a baronet and Old Etonian. During his time as a diplomat he had served in a number of countries, including Spain, and was an acknowledged expert on the county and its people. As he followed the ongoing tragedy engulfing a country to which he felt such close bonds, the philanthropic Sir George resolved to use his own funds and contacts to create a voluntary ambulance unit and personally take it to Spain. This venture would become known as the George Young Ambulance Unit, otherwise known as the University Ambulance Unit, named for its main sponsors – representatives of British universities – and go on to save untold numbers of lives in Spain.

Preoccupied as he was by attempts to obtain visas, raise funds and locate trained medical personnel, Sir George had recently been presented with an unforeseen complication. Two Spanish girls who worked for him and Lady Young in London had suddenly announced their decision to return to their families in Torremolinos, where Sir George owned a large house. Given the circumstances, Sir George was reluctant to allow the girls to travel home alone. Hostility from the rebels towards him and his wife meant Lady Young was not in a position to travel as far as Spain with the servants. He therefore urgently needed to find a reliable chaperone. But where, he asked himself, would he find a woman who not only spoke Spanish but was also willing to escort two strangers through a warzone where civilians, regarded by the rebels as legitimate targets, were dying in their thousands? Fortunately, one of Sir George's contacts introduced him to the ideal candidate – a 28-year-old Irishwoman named Mary Elmes, who worked at Chatham House, the respected international affairs think tank. Tall and imposing, this quietly capable, confident young woman had a brilliant academic record, spoke fluent Spanish and French, and was already a seasoned European traveller.

Mary Elmes was born into a well-to-do, non-practising Protestant family in Cork on 5 May 1908 as Marie Elisabeth Jane Elmes. Her parents, Edward and Elisabeth, owed a pharmacy on the city's Winthrop Street and she lived with her parents and younger brother, John, in Ballintemple, on the south side of the River Lee. Her family had a number of military connections – an uncle had been killed in the Boer War Battle of Ladysmith in 1899 and later a cousin served in the Indian Army. Perhaps it was these family links that inspired Mary, at the age of nine, to play her own modest role in the First World War effort by knitting socks and sending them to General Sir John French, commander of the British Army during the First World War Battle of the Marne, to distribute among his men. By way of thanks, Sir John sent the young Mary a signed portrait, a gift she kept for more than 50 years until it was stolen in a burglary from her home in France.

As a child Mary had frequently expressed an ambition to become a doctor. By the time she graduated from university, however, her interest had switched to international affairs. At one point she hoped to follow a career in the diplomatic service. In 1915 Mary enrolled in the local Rochelle School, known today as Ashton School. At the age of nineteen she showed a glimpse of the self-reliance and independence that would later serve her well when she set off on an extended tour of Europe. By 1926 she had travelled through Switzerland, Italy, Spain and France. On her return to Ireland she enrolled in Trinity College Dublin in June 1928 to study Modern Literature (French and Spanish), becoming a Scholar of the university in 1931, an achievement, then as now, reserved for students of exceptional academic ability. The following year she graduated with First Class Honours and, as top student for her year, won the Gold Medal. Coincidentally, five years earlier, her compatriot, the playwright and Noble Laureate Samuel Beckett, had preceded her as a TCD Scholar in Modern Literature (French and Italian), before also graduating with a First. Years later in wartime France the names of both she and Beckett, who never met, featured on the list of those being hunted down by the Gestapo – he for his work with the French Resistance, she for helping Jews escape deportation.

Following a recommendation from her professor, Francis la Touche Godfrey, Mary was awarded a scholarship of £30 a year from TCD to the London School of Economics (LSE), where she studied for a Certificate in International Studies. Typically, her final results earned her a second scholarship – this time from the LSE to attend the Geneva School of International Studies' one-month summer school.

Mary's European travels and her time in London had broadened her outlook and thrust her into an environment where intellectual debate flourished – a far remove from the narrow, conservative worldview that prevailed in her home country. Perhaps not surprisingly, although she frequently visited Ireland while her mother and brother were alive, she never returned to live there permanently.

From her base in London Mary and her friends kept a keen eye on contemporary European affairs, where the twin evils of fascism and the rise of the Nazis provided a daily digest for discussion. Of her time in the LSE she recalled, "There were no fascists there! … [T]hey even had a committee that was anti-Franco", adding, "I was interested in politics. Not that I was in any way political."

Around this time Mary first met Edith Pye, a well-known British Quaker who had been awarded the Légion d'Honneur by France for her humanitarian work during the First World War and was now helping to coordinate Quaker relief efforts in Spain via the Friends Service Council (FSC).

"Miss Pye was one of the directors of Friends House [the Quaker headquarters] in London. A much more important person than me. I had met her in London before the war, when I was thinking of going to help in Spain. … She was a great woman who had been in the First World War. … Miss Pye was already in the Spanish war network", Mary later told one interviewer.

The FSC involvement in Spanish relief work began just a few weeks after the Francoist military coup, when the British-American Quaker couple Alfred and Norma Noble travelled to Barcelona to set up a mission. At this stage Barcelona was still under Republican control and, at least for the moment, still a safe distance from the frontlines. The couple's arrival coincided with that of the first wave of refugees fleeing areas taken over by the Nationalist rebels – a scenario that would become a regular feature of the conflict. Faced with hundreds of starving people the Nobles altered their original plan and instead set up a feeding station for children. From this modest beginning grew a flourishing Quaker network that would provide thousands of meals and milk to the most needy. The Quakers, who together with other aid agencies provided shelter and sustenance throughout the years of war in Spain, continued their service in France, when almost half a million Spaniards fled over the Pyrenees when the Republican defeat became inevitable.

Another strand of relief was provided by the National Joint Committee for Spanish Relief (NJCSR) – a British voluntary grouping formed after a visit to Madrid, Valencia and Barcelona by a group of six all-party MPs in November 1936. On their return to London the MPs organised a meeting at Friends House in December and the following month the committee met for the first time. The committee became an umbrella organisation, streamlining the work of the various humanitarian groups in Spain. In Britain the organisation launched a number of initiatives to raise funds and awareness of Spain's plight among the British population. These included organising talks, concerts and exhibitions – one of which, in London in October 1938, displayed Picasso's painting *Guernica*, commemorating the previous year's massacre of an estimated 1,600 civilians in the Basque city by bombers from the German Condor Legion.

In the immediate aftermath of the fascist coup the Republicans sought support from the left-wing French Government led by Léon Blum. Although Blum initially favoured offering assistance to his Republican neighbours by providing warplanes and weapons, he quickly came under pressure to reverse this stance from British Prime Minister Stanley Baldwin and the more right-wing members of his own Cabinet. Fearful that the conflict would seep over the border into France or that support for the Republicans from Paris would provoke military retaliation from fascist Italy or Nazi Germany on its eastern borders, Blum joined his British counterparts in urging all European countries against intervention in the Spanish conflict. In the event, 27 countries, including Ireland, signed the Non-Intervention Pact, a pathetic fiction that allowed Hitler and Mussolini – both signatories of the pact – to continue supplying arms, warplanes and troops to Francisco Franco's Nationalist rebels. The Soviet Union, also a signatory to the pact, provided weapons and 'advisors' to the Republican side. US President Franklin D. Roosevelt, although not a signatory of the pact, made it known that his government also favoured non-intervention. Sir George poured scorn on the official British stance on Spain, which he believed had left Britain "in the position of a policeman who had ceased to uphold the law".

Even as the world drifted inexorably towards the wider war that would engulf it in a few years, the Western powers clung to the belief that peace could be best preserved by confining the conflict in Spain within its borders. But by pushing for a non-intervention pact, Britain and France had created a policy that effectively abandoned the democratically elected Republican Government while tacitly supporting its fascist enemies. As a strategy it was both cowardly and misguided and allowed Hitler to enact in Spain a deadly dress rehearsal for the Blitzkrieg tactics of carpet-bombing cities he would later deploy when full-scale war descended on the continent. A secondary benefit, from Hitler's point of view, was that the outrage provoked by murderous attacks on Spanish civilians distracted attention from his own machinations further east.

The Nationalists' policy of bombing cities and towns to inflict maximum civilian casualties – the first deployment of the tactic in modern warfare – was unleashed shortly after the outbreak of the war in July 1936 with the help of German and Italian warplanes. In the face of these deadly new tactics, Spain's medical system quickly collapsed under the weight of the escalating numbers of wounded civilians and the subsequent outbreaks of infectious diseases among the displaced and starving survivors.

Despite the Non-Intervention Pact's abandonment of the Republic, the Spanish Civil War prompted an unprecedented wave of international solidarity. A massive fundraising and relief effort was complemented militarily by the creation of the International Brigades, which saw thousands of volunteers from more than fifty different countries risk their lives to fight to preserve the Republic. In its two-year existence from late 1936 to December 1938, more than 35,000 volunteers served in the Brigades, at least 15,000 of whom sacrificed their lives for the Republican cause.

In London, Mary Elmes, regardless of her own country's position on non-intervention, was determined to travel to Spain to help in the relief work and was about to resign from Chatham House when Sir George approached her. "They knew that I spoke Spanish. They asked me to accompany Lady Young as far as Gibraltar. I was sent by her to Torremolinos", she recalled.

Despite their willingness to place themselves in harm's way, Mary and the rest of Sir George's party were under no illusions about the scale of the danger into which they were heading. On 6 February 1937, just days before Mary set off for Spain, Sir George's supporters published a harrowing update of the situation in the British press:

> Casualties have been very heavy and will become heavier on these confused Andalusian fronts, isolated from the rest of Spain by a hundred miles of mountain roads.
>
> In these remote ranges wounded are now often being abandoned to exposure, gangrene, or the more merciful bayonet.

The article went on to appeal for field ambulances, trained nurses, doctors and medical supplies. A report in the *Manchester Guardian* continued the theme:

> Now that Malaga has fallen the war will move into this wild and mountainous region, where roads are few and valleys generally barren and waterless. The sufferings of the wounded in this sparsely inhabited country are likely to be even greater than they

> have been in other parts of Spain. The Government has lost in Malaga its ambulances, its medical supplies, and a large staff of doctors and nurses. Almeria, a small city with few resources, will be quite unable to take care of any number of wounded adequately. It is at a point where even a small amount of efficient outside help can be of inestimable value in relieving the horrible suffering caused by war.

By the middle of February, just a week after the fall of Malaga, an ambulance and two cars carrying Sir George and a group of volunteers left Britain for Spain, travelling overland via the French port of Dieppe.

Sir George's party included four qualified nurses, one of whom was Dorothy Morris from Christchurch, New Zealand. Forceful, courageous and dedicated to those in her care, Dorothy had much in common with Mary Elmes and, not surprisingly, within a short time the two women became firm friends. The pair went on to work side by side – first in Spain and later on the other side of the Pyrenees in France. The University Ambulance Unit's commandant was Violetta Thurstan, a veteran relief worker who had served as a nurse and administrator during the First World War.

Two days after the departure of Sir George and his party, Mary and Lady Young sailed for Gibraltar with supplies for the unit. Mary's instructions were to ensure that these supplies were to be docked in Spain ahead of Sir George's arrival. Lady Young was to base herself in Gibraltar to coordinate the provision of further supplies to the unit. Mary's original plan was to embark for Malaga aboard the Royal Navy destroyer HMS *Boadicea*, see her two charges safely home to Torremolinos and continue on to Malaga with the unit's initial batch of supplies. Queipo de Llano's onslaught against Malaga meant the British destroyer could no longer safely dock there so the ship changed course for Almeria. *Boadicea* went on to play a leading role in the arms blockade imposed by France and Britain against both sides in the Spanish conflict before being sunk by German dive-bombers in 1944 with heavy loss of life.

When Mary stepped ashore off the *Boadicea*'s gangplank she was confronted by a scene of utter chaos as thousands of terrified and hungry survivors of the Caravan of Death frantically sought food and shelter in a city whose own citizens were already on the verge of starvation and enduring daily bombing raids.

Violetta Thurstan, who had arrived in Almeria a few days ahead of Mary, urgently wrote to Lady Young in Gibraltar pleading that delivery of the unit's supplies be expedited:

> Food is terribly short, there are long queues of people waiting for bread and yesterday the [shop] doors were shut because there was no more and women with little babies had to go away crying. They say there is scarcely any more food in Almeria and begged me to send you a telegram in case it is possible for you to send a few supplies by sea. … We thought that if we set up a feeding station with a surgery attached it would save many lives.

Violetta went on to say that "a bomb has just gone off and the streets are so crowded that everyone gets into a panic", before closing on a hopeful note: "I am very glad I came. If only I can relieve a little bit the awful suffering that is going on all around me".

When Lady Young and Mary left Britain they took with them a cargo of six and a half tons of rice, potatoes, beans, flour, soap, bandages and disinfectants. The NJCRS had donated £50 worth of milk and a further £100 which Lady Young used to buy additional food supplies in Gibraltar. Mary and her cargo docked in Almeria on the same day as Sir George's party arrived in the city, enabling him to immediately establish a feeding station for refugees in the station square, even before organising accommodation for the unit's members. The feeding station supplied milk to children and the sick in the morning and soup to all-comers every afternoon. In a letter Sir George described the fraught situation in the city: "The place is full of refugees from Malaga and the surrounding villages, who welcomed us with such joy and terrible stories", he wrote.

> One woman had her small boy shot, but saved the little girls. … Almeria is bombarded every morning pretty well and the anti-aircraft battery replies. … The cellars of this house are packed

> full of refugees living on bread and water and even the water is rationed. Some of them are ill and we are planning to start a sort of ward in a shed near the feeding station. However, the peak is passed and the villagers this side of the line are returning to the mountains, leaving only those from Malaga and the West. One family of small children had walked or run all the way from Ronda and then from Malaga without food.

As Mary later explained, Sir George had originally planned to open field hospitals on the frontlines to care for the wounded on both sides of the conflict. However, a meeting with representatives of the Republican Government convinced him that the thousands of children suffering from malnutrition and disease were more urgently in need of the unit's services.

In London Sir George had worked closely with the British Quakers while setting up his ambulance unit. Once on Spanish soil he made contact with their American counterparts, the American Friends Service Committee (AFSC), to whom he eventually handed over the administration of his ambulance unit when his own funds were depleted.

Mary had arrived in Almeria carrying a visa that was valid for just five days. Sir George, it seems, expected her to return to London immediately after safely delivering his servants to their homes. As usual, however, this strong-willed Irishwoman had plans of her own and regardless of the dangers was determined to stay in Spain for as long as she could help. On 17 March 1937, Violetta Thurstan wrote to Edith Pye in London updating her on the unit's progress. In a comment that must have rekindled in the veteran Pye memories of her own early days as a relief worker in the Great War, Violeta added that "… a worker came from Gibraltar, Miss Elmes, and I gave the feeding station to her." Mary's career as a humanitarian aid worker had begun.

***

The Friends' contribution to Spanish relief efforts was enormous: between 1936 and 1942 British and American Quaker relief workers with whom Mary worked provided food and clothing for 150,000 children in Republican and Nationalist Spain, having expanded their operations from their initial base in Barcelona.

As Mary later recalled, "We had a lot of children who were ill because there was a famine in Spain at that time. Sir George kept sending us food. When it became beyond him the AFSC took over and all our money and supplies came from them."

A fundraising pamphlet published by the British Friends in 1937 describes another important element of their work:

> One of the most constructive forms of relief at the present time is the setting up of Children's Colonies. Large country houses standing empty have been taken over and adapted into homes or colonies for the children. The Spanish authorities have established many, and the Friends have been responsible for the setting up of others. … Here the children are cared for by responsible people and go on with their schooling.

For Mary, the experience of seeing firsthand the creation and day-to-day running of these colonies was to prove invaluable years later in France, first as a way of temporarily arranging for children to be cared for outside the internment camps and later when the deportations of Jews to the death camps began and she was desperately searching for places to hide children destined for the transports.

In Spain, meanwhile, a number of organisations cooperated with each other to maximise their relief efforts. These included the Save the Children Fund and Save the Children International Union. Another group providing assistance were the Mennonites, a Christian denomination dedicated, like the Quakers, to pacifism and with whose representative in France, Lois Gunden, Mary would work in the dark days of 1942.

In Switzerland, Service Civil International (SCI) created a Committee of Swiss Aid to Children to provide humanitarian support in Spain. On 27 April 1937, four trucks carrying twelve SCI volunteers rolled into Spain and set up base in Burjassot in Valencia, north of Alicante, and immediately set about helping to evacuate women, children and the elderly from Madrid, as well as establishing feeding stations.

Sir George's first children's hospital in Almeria was based in a house named Villa Maria and had the use of a number of 'ambulances' – vehicles which had originally been destined for the frontlines. The villa was just one of many such properties which had been abandoned by their wealthy owners and could be occupied for a nominal rent or sometimes none at all. The hospital catered exclusively for children and the staff included Mary, Dorothy Morris, Spanish paediatrician Manuel Blanc and a dozen English nurses. The Communist Governor of Alicante, Jésus Monzón, who had been appointed in July 1937, knew Sir George and had close links to Dr Blanc. He proved to be a powerful local supporter of the unit. Monzón was born into a wealthy family in Pamplona in 1910 and after studying in Barcelona and Madrid qualified as a lawyer. Monzón joined the Communist Party of Spain but his affluent background sparked suspicion and he struggled for acceptance from his colleagues, several of whom doubted his motives in joining the party and even suspected him of being a spy. After Franco's victory in March 1939 he was lucky to escape from Spain aboard a small plane carrying other senior communist figures, including Dolores Ibárruri, known as La Pasionaria, whose impassioned frontline speeches had aroused such patriotic inspiration among those fighting for the Republic. Despite encountering enemy gunfire on take-off, Monzón and his colleagues landed safely in the French colonial port of Oran in Algeria, from where he made his way to France. When France was invaded by Germany in June 1942 he helped arrange for Republican fighters interned in the Pyrenees-Orientales to join the Resistance movement. In 1943 he secretly returned to Spain and began plotting to invade his homeland using some of these Spanish fighters. Monzón hoped that this invasion – which took place in October 1944 – would draw the Allies into a confrontation with the Nationalists and ultimately lead to Franco's overthrow and the re-establishment of the Republic. When the invasion ended in abject failure, Monzón became further isolated from party members and found himself abandoned by the Spanish Communist leadership. A planned return to France was thwarted by his arrest in Barcelona in 1945. He was sentenced to thirty years in prison, only avoiding execution because of friends who had influence with the Nationalist Government. Monzón was eventually released in 1959 and spent several years living on the Balearic Islands before returning to Pamplona shortly before his death in 1973.

In May the hospital temporarily relocated to another house, Villa Elena, for three weeks before transferring to Murcia. By this stage Mary's organisational skills and ability to rapidly adapt to the evolving conditions had come to the notice of her superiors, who put her in charge of their children's hospital in Alicante, a short distance along the coast from Murcia. She held this post for two years until the Republican defeat in 1939 and, despite the risk of brutal reprisals by Nationalist forces, remained at the hospital, quitting her post only when she felt she could be more useful on the French side of the border. In her typically understated way she later referred to the fraught period before leaving Spain simply as being "very uncomfortable".

Although donations from Sir George, his supporters in Britain and the Quakers ensured that the Alicante hospital was kept well-equipped, its coastal location left it prey to daily bombardment from the sea, forcing the terrified young patients and staff to take refuge in the basement as shells exploded above their heads. Mary began scouting out the area and eventually located a replacement property ten miles inland in the small hilltown of Polop. Dorothy Litten, one of the nurses who later worked there, described it in a letter to Friends House in 1938:

> The hospital is now settled in the summer residence of a rich man who has fled to a more suitable spot for rich men. The land is being farmed by five peasants but the house stood empty and really makes a surprisingly good hospital. The rooms are a bit crowded but that does not matter now that the children are out all day, and perhaps before winter it will be possible to return to Alicante.

The letter went on to say that 23 children had been moved to Polop from Alicante and praised Mary's resourcefulness in managing to provide a steady supply of nourishing meals despite the scarcity of food.

In the event, the hospital remained in Polop until the end of the fighting. In a letter to her family in New Zealand, written in January 1939 shortly before the Republican defeat, Dorothy Morris wrote:

> Next week I may have a short time off and go to our other hospital run by my friend Mary Elmes – did I tell you about it? They had a beautiful hospital running in Alicante but the bombing drove them out to a hill village – rather remote but beautiful, with clear sparkling air and quiet. Their doctor brings the children by car from clinics amongst the refugees along the coast.

In a later letter she describes the hospital as:

> ... a small square white country house, 'a finch', a rather Moorish looking building, has about 35 children, mostly convalescent from their ills and running about in the lovely sun. It is run by my friend Mary Elmes ... an Irish England [sic] girl, very calm, collected and capable who came to us in Almeria nearly two years ago. ... She is giving me a heavenly restful holiday.

The importance of staff taking rest periods away from the hospital frequently features in correspondence between Friends House and the aid workers, whose duties not only required outstanding physical stamina but were also emotionally draining. For at least one of Mary's nurses the constant strain provoked a physical and nervous breakdown which forced Mary to declare her unfit for duty and to order her back to London. One particularly poignant aspect of their duties was recalled in 2012 when Mary's daughter, Caroline Danjou, made a journey to Polop. One elderly lady in the village told her how she remembered young nurses in their white uniforms regularly making their way to the local cemetery with wicker baskets or powdered milk cartons carrying the bodies of infants they had been unable to save. Nor were the deaths confined to infants, as Mary recalled: "At Polop we also had a group of older boys sent by the hospital in Madrid. They ... had been moved away from the bombing. They were all very ill and some of them died despite our care."

In January 1938 Mary learnt by telegram that her father had died in Ireland. Her mother, unnerved by reports of the war and the atrocities being perpetrated by both sides of the conflict, begged her to return home. But with a number of exhausted nurses on leave the hospital was barely coping with its young patients and since there was no one to replace her Mary resisted her mother's entreaties and remained at her post.

In February 1938, Emily Parker of the AFSC gave voice to her thoughts in an emotional letter in which she reflected on the futility of war:

> … a waste one can hardly comprehend, though looking at these babies in our hospitals, or watching them being carried out, sometimes two and three a day in little coffins made from powered milk cartons … or seeing children faint as they stand in line waiting for the bit we have to have to give.

Decades later Mary came close to tears as she reflected on the human cost of warfare: "War is a terrible thing, which is never won. It's always lost. Everybody loses."

Although the hospital catered mainly for children suffering from malnutrition and diseases such as typhus, TB and skin disorders, it also nursed young victims of war. One such patient was an infant called Palmira Sanchez. On 25 May 1938 she and her parents were rambling through Alicante's bustling central market searching for food when a squadron of bombers from Italy's Aviazione Legionaria suddenly loomed over the city. The attack, one of the deadliest air raids of the war, killed some 300 civilians and injured more than 1,000 as 90 high explosive bombs rained down on the defenceless city. Palmira, whose father had been standing some distance away from her, was blasted from her mother's arms. Bleeding profusely after sustaining serious injuries to her left leg, the child was ferried to the nearest hospital, which by then was over-flowing with the wounded and dying. Amid the chaos and carnage the overworked surgeons felt they had no option but to amputate the child's leg. The eventual outcome, as Mary recalled in a 1998 letter to her friend Rose Duroux, was rather more fortuitous:

> Have I spoken to you about Palmira? She was a pretty child of twenty-one months, wounded in the bombing of Alicante market in 1938. Her mother was holding her in her arms at the time. In the confusion that followed she lost her child. Very badly injured in the left leg, with her foot just hanging on by a few shreds of skin. The overworked surgeons wanted to cut off her foot. Fortunately, the doctor from our little hospital, a paediatrician [Dr Blanc], was against this and took her to our place where she was immobilized on a plank for three months, at the end of which she could stand and eventually walk normally. It was a triumph for Dr Blanc and the English nurses, whose devotion and patience is to be admired.
>
> Being so young she couldn't tell us who she was and her family didn't find her for several days – oh such tears of joy when her father finally found her.

Of all the children that Mary cared for, one little Spanish orphan boy, whose name no one knew, held an enduring place in her heart.

> He was lost ... we called him Tato. He didn't know who he was. He was only about two or three. Didn't know anything about himself or where he lived or anything. When we left, we took him back to one of these Spanish colonies where they took him on. He was a charming little boy. I became very attached to that child but we couldn't keep him.
>
> We never knew his real name because he was so young he couldn't tell us. We kept him for two years. At one time I wanted to adopt him but I was too young – you had to be forty-five to adopt a child and my mother, who was ill, didn't feel that she could take on that responsibility.

Sir George, who had returned to Britain late in 1937, was obviously aware of Mary's attachment to Tato, as indicated in a letter voicing his concerns about the need for the ongoing treatment of the hospitals' young patients following the rebel victory. Writing to Dorothy Thomson of the Friends Spain Committee in London in April 1939, soon after the Republican defeat, he outlined his plans:

> The suggestion I had in mind about the Murcia and Polop hospitals was this –
>
> The Malaga refugees at Alicante and Murcia who mostly benefitted by them will now be returning to their own province. On the other hand the proprietor of the Murcia building will now be recovering his property and the hospital may get very short notice to evacuate. The same will happen more politely at Polop.
>
> I suggest therefore that both hospitals, with their equipment and such patients as are suitable, be transferred to my large house at Malaga which Mary Elmes knows – and be continued there for six months or if necessary for a year, for the benefit of Malaga (six miles). There is an excellent doctor at Torremolinos, a large children's sanatorium for Central Spain two miles away, and a good consul at Malaga. Communications are by bus from Gibraltar (four hours).

In the event however, Sir George's offer came to nothing as Nationalist antagonism to the Quakers eventually forced Mary and her colleagues out of Spain.

That same month, shortly after the fall of Barcelona to the Nationalists, Dorothy Morris received a letter from Friends House instructing her to leave Spain. With Franco's victory all but certain her superiors had strong grounds to fear for her safety: at one stage of her career in Spain Dorothy had nursed wounded members of the International Brigades. In the eyes of the Nationalists this proved she had given succour to the enemy and was therefore liable to be executed. She later vented her frustration when she wrote:

> I left only because I had to! It was considered that my life and liberty were in danger owing to the probable change of regime.

> Franco and his fellow murderers hated the International Brigade – because they were such fine soldiers and blocked him for so long – so that anyone connected with them has been threatened with much ferocity. And I of course 2 years ago did a lot of work for the Brigade. As the German secret police – the Gestapo – are expected to start work right away on Nazi models, the Quakers became alarmed for my safety in case I should be arrested! Imagine – for nursing sick men!

In late 1938, amid a seemingly endless flood of refugees fleeing the advance of Nationalist forces, a multinational organisation was established to coordinate and disburse the various funds being donated to the humanitarian agencies. This new organisation, to be known as the International Commission for the Assistance of Spanish Child Refugees, was the brainchild of a number of prominent British Quakers – among them the redoubtable Edith Pye – who prevailed upon the leaders of a total of 24 countries in Europe and beyond to create it. The International Commission, as it became known, set itself the task of providing every needy Spanish child with one hot, nutritional meal a day. The task of distributing grain and other foodstuffs supplied by the Commission was taken on by both the FSC and the AFSC. In mid-1938 the FSC's standing in Spain and abroad benefitted from the Commission's decision that henceforth it would provide most of the British Quakers' funding, thus affording them official status by association. In a letter to her family, the New Zealander Dorothy Morris wrote:

> The International Commission … is using the Quakers amongst others in Spain for the organisation and supervision of canteens for the distribution of chocolate and milk. In addition the American Govt has given an enormous quantity of flour – 75,000 tons or more … which will be distributed as bread (if it isn't sunk at the ports – however the Americans have warned Mr Franco and so far USA ships are comparatively immune).

2

Retirada

By the end of 1938, with victory for the Nationalist forces increasingly likely, thousands of Republicans began making their way across the border with France. The fall of Catalonia in January 1939 prompted ever greater numbers of refugees to join those in flight. Behind them trudged demoralised, routed Republican army soldiers, many of whom were clinging to hopes of regrouping on the other side of the border to carry on the fight against fascism. This desperate flood of humanity would become known as the Retirada or Retreat – a movement of people on a scale not witnessed since the expulsion of the Moors from Spain in the Middle Ages. During the first two weeks of February 1939 more than 450,000 men, women and children struggled over the Pyrenees to France, most travelling on foot in icy rain or snow, frequently under fire from German and Italian aircraft.

"The immensity of the tragedy of the flight from Spain must have been seen at first hand to be believed", wrote Edith Pye in her report on the Retirada for the International Commission.

> The bombardments from the air forced the inhabitants to leave the ruins of their houses, and the descent of the aeroplanes almost to roof level to machine gun the fleeing inhabitants left them no choice.
>
> For days, while only a meagre trickle of civilians were allowed to pass the frontier, there were literally hundreds standing in queues between one village and another, or camped without any

shelter on the hillsides on each side of the roads to the frontier in deadly fear of bombardments from the air. …

Of these border posts there are three in which there is a road through – Port Bou/Cebere, Puigcerda/Bourg Madame, La Jonquera/Le Perthus. There is also a road on the Spanish side but only mountain paths at Prats de Mollo which is above the snow line, and there were pitiful cases of women and children lost in a snowstorm and being picked up half frozen. Intellectuals and peasants suffered alike, the latter perhaps less since many of them had brought their mules and bread with them. Some had a sheep or two tied by a string, here and there one saw a cow or goats, and even hens carried by their legs, as uncomplaining as their owners. The first three nights there was heavy rain in which it was stated there were many deaths from exposure, especially among the children and the wounded.

There was no shelter of any kind available. The French authorities by a tremendous feat of organization succeeded in getting 45,000 women and children sent into the interior in the first three days. They were brought down, after several days on the frontier with no possibility of washing or of proper food, in lorries or buses, vaccinated, and sent off in trainloads to destinations unknown. The separation from their menfolk produced despair among the refugees.

But many thousands more spent another five nights on the hillsides on the French side. The misery and helplessness of these crowds, harried by French cavalry to keep them from straying, is indescribable.

Despite the likelihood of just such an influx of their Spanish neighbours, the French authorities had made scant preparations other than making sure they had sufficient military manpower to secure the border crossings. As the numbers of people massing at these crossings headed for half a million the decision was made to close the frontier to the refugees. With hundreds of people – a third of whom were women, children or the elderly – arriving by the hour this decision simply created a pathetic, ever-increasing human tailback. Finally, after enduring days of waiting by the roadside in the freezing rain, the refugees were allowed to cross into France. But not before the International Brigadists and Republican troops had been made to surrender their weapons, which were left in piles at the border crossings. After their long years of struggle against fascism the Republicans massed at the border might have expected at least a show of international solidarity from their French neighbours. But the mood of xenophobia that had taken hold in France meant outsiders were feared and unwelcome. In fact the French authorities, faced with logistical chaos and a pathological fear of political contagion from the Communists among the starving refugees, hoped to persuade as many of them as possible to return to Spain, regardless of the consequences.

Gustav Regler, a German Communist commissar with the International Brigades, arrived at the French frontier looking for some of his men, who were among the last to cross the frontier. He wrote afterwards:

> That afternoon the Republican troops came. They were received as though they were tramps. The Spaniards were asked what was in their haversacks and ditty bags they carried and they answered that in surrendering their rifles they had given them all the arms they possessed. But the French tapped disdainfully on the haversacks and demanded that they should be opened. The Spaniards did not understand. Until the last moment they insisted in believing in the tragic error of believing in international solidarity. The dirty road on which the disarmed men stood was not merely the frontier between two countries – it was an abyss between two worlds. Under the eyes of the prefect and the generals the men of the Gardes Mobiles took away the bags containing the Spaniards' personal belongings and emptied their contents into a ditch filled with chloride of lime. I have never seen eyes of such anger and helplessness as those of the Spaniards. They stood as though turned to stone.

For Spanish Republicans, France's decision to sign the Non-Intervention Pact and refuse them the weapons needed to defend themselves represented a grand betrayal of their ideals. Now they were being spurned a second time by being treated as unwanted outcasts. In his book *The 186 Steps*, Christian Bernadac wrote:

> They were Republican soldiers who had come across the French frontier in February 1939, after the fall of Catalonia. They hoped to build their strength, regroup, train and leave for the other side of the Pyrenees, where genuine pockets of resistance still held out. They arrived with arms and baggage and all this good material rotted on the snow-covered mountain passes or the wet slopes of the Mediterranean. …
>
> And they, the vanquished serfs, were herded into improvised 'transit' camps, where they died, literally, of hunger, cold and dysentery.

A third betrayal by France saw thousands of these men, who had been enrolled in work companies or irregular battalions of foreign volunteers, handed over to the Nazis to work – and die – as slave labourers in the Austrian concentration camp of Mauthausen. It has been estimated that of the 8,000 Spanish Republicans sent to the camp only 800 survived.

In her book *Love and War in the Pyrenees*, Rosemary Bailey quotes Jose Sangenis, who was twelve years old when he and his family joined the Retirada: "My father, my mother, my sister a year older than me, we left on foot, with the planes behind us, flying at low altitude, shooting unarmed civilians. I will never, never forget it."

After being forced to wait at Le Perthus with thousands of fellow refugees, the family were sent to Le Boulou, where they camped beside the river. "It was snowing, and we only had one blanket each to protect us from the cold. I still remember it now whenever it snows, I feel those tears of cold again."

***

In the midst of this chaos the Quakers continued to provide relief to those thronging the mountain roads. A cable sent to Friends House on

30 January 1939 by Edith Pye recounts how Quaker aid workers had been bombed out of Girona, between Barcelona and the French frontier. All were safe and had managed to organise emergency canteens to provide hot milk and bread to refugees. Conditions on the road were dreadful, she wrote, often choked with refugees and impassable for miles.

Once on French soil these starving, dejected people were subjected to even further indignities. Families were separated from one another as women and children were dispersed to be housed inland while the men were herded into internment 'camps'. At this point the so-called camps were nothing more than areas on the sand enclosed by barbed wire along the beaches of Languedoc-Roussillon, such as Argelès-sur-Mer. Here the Republicans were held with nothing between them and the freezing weather but the clothes they arrived in. About 30,000 of the men were nursing war wounds that had become gangrenous and for which they had only field dressings to treat them. Without a roof to protect them from the winter rain and no walls to shelter them from the relentless icy blast of the Tramontane wind hurtling down from the snow-capped mountains, many desperately dug holes in the freezing sand and huddled down in them to find some small shelter, or made hovels from driftwood and scraps of fabric.

Initially there were no latrines so the sea and sand were used as toilets, in full view of everyone else. No medical or washing facilities were provided and not surprisingly the water supply quickly became contaminated.

Possibly seeking to distance themselves from this affront to human dignity, the French authorities mainly deployed colonial troops from Senegal to supervise the refugees inside the barbed wire, their uniforms and appearance eerie reminders of Queipo de Llano's brutal Moorish forces. These Senegalese troops, usually mounted on horses and exulting in the exercise of power over others for the first time in their lives, were quick to use their whips or the backs of their swords to control the bedraggled, starving inmates. In the first weeks the food distribution consisted of the guards simply throwing bread over the wire, prompting a frantic free-for-all among those trapped inside.

By 6 February 1939 there were 20,000 refugees in the camp at Argelès. Two days later the number had reached 60,000 and by the beginning of March the figure had swelled to 100,000. That same month the war photographer Robert Capa, who had covered the conflict in Spain, was sent on assignment to Argelès. Capa was horrified to see men who had fought so hard to preserve their Republic penned in behind barbed wire as though they were wild animals. The scenes he captured show these once proud soldiers forced to live in burrows in the sand or in flimsy, makeshift shelters in what he called "a hell on the sand".

By late spring, as the surge of refugees continued, the authorities opened another camp further along the coast at St Cyprien in early February. Within a few weeks it held 95,000 men. A third camp followed at Barcarès, twenty miles north of Argelès. In a pattern that was to be tragically repeated again and again, the camp at Barcarès, originally designed to accommodate 13,000 refugees, soon found the number of its inmates had risen to more than 50,000. Before long infectious diseases such as dysentery, pneumonia and tuberculosis began to spread through the camps. Yet it was weeks before the authorities, unwilling to reveal the scale of suffering they had helped create, agreed to grant aid workers access to the refugees. When the Quaker doctor Audrey Russell, who had worked with Mary Elmes and Dorothy Morris in Murcia, finally succeeded in gaining entry to Argelès she reported that "there has never been anything as horrible as this since the Middle Ages." Francesca Wilson, another of Mary's colleagues in Spain, first visited Argelès in February 1939. Her reaction was unequivocal: "I wanted to cover my eyes – it was so wounding to human dignity. Men penned in cages like animals; exposed to the stare of the passer-by, like cattle in the market place."

World-famous Catalan cellist Pablo Casals was living in self-imposed exile in the nearby town of Prades close to the Spanish border. After his first visit to the camps he wrote despairingly to a friend:

> There are no words to describe the horror of what is going on here. The scenes I witnessed might have been from Dante's *Inferno*. Tens of thousands of men, women and children were herded together

> like animals, penned in by barbed wire, housed – if one can call it that – in tents and crumbling shacks. There are no sanitation facilities or provisions for medical care. There was little water and barely enough food to keep the inmates from starvation. The camp at Argelès was typical. Here more than a hundred thousand refugees had been massed in open areas among sand dunes along the seashore. Though it was winter they had been provided with no shelter whatsoever – many had burrowed holes in the wet sand to protect themselves from the pelting rain and bitter winds. The driftwood they gathered for fires to warm themselves was soon exhausted. Scores had perished from exposure, hunger and disease. At the time of my arrival the hospitals in Perpignan still overflowed with the sick and dying.

Casals, an outspoken critic of Franco, had been warned by Franco's generals that his arms would be cut off at the elbows if he ever returned to Spain. He and Mary became close friends and the pair worked together for years to help the refugees, with Casals staging concerts to raise funds to buy food and other essentials as well as using his celebrity to heighten awareness outside of France of the terrible reality of the camps.

***

In Spain the last acts of the war were being played out. Barcelona fell to the Nationalists in January and on 28 March 1939 Franco's forces marched triumphantly into Madrid. On 1 April Franco declared victory. The war was over but the task of caring for the hundreds of displaced and starving refugees left in its wake was far from finished. Every day another wave of bedraggled and desperate people joined those already stranded at the frontier. Although some of her colleagues had joined the Retirada, Mary chose to remain in Alicante for the time being and had taken over the running of temporary canteens, which had originally been set up by Dorothy Morris, to distribute food and milk. This role had been a central plank in Quaker relief efforts since the outbreak of the conflict, but while Mary and her colleagues struggled to cope in this latest phase of the conflict, Franco's forces were pursuing a more bloodthirsty agenda – rounding up and killing surviving Republicans in their thousands. In Alicante itself more than 6,000 Republicans crammed into the port in a desperate bid to escape by sea. Sir George had come to assist Spaniards shortly after the outbreak of the civil war; now, with the fighting entering its closing stage, the indefatigable former diplomat was back in Spain, having returned on 27 March as part of the recently created International Delegation to Spain for Relief and Evacuation of Refugees. The delegation's mission was to negotiate the safe passage of those trapped in the port. Once again, British and French intransigence stymied the delegation's efforts to fulfil its brief and the men trapped in the port fell victim to yet another massacre. Just 650 Republicans managed to escape, with many of those left behind electing to die by their own hand rather than face capture. Amid the chaos Mary struggled to ensure that the hospital in nearby Polop continued to function, albeit uneasily, under the new regime.

"I was there up until the end of the fighting. All our jobs were taken over brutally by Franco and his friends when they got in. We had stocks and they just came and took it without asking", she recalled.

Mary's situation was not unlike that of nurses Sylvia Pitt and Rachel Marshall at the hospital in Murcia at the end of the fighting:

> The canteens were re-staffed with Fascist girls, but continued to use our food. The 26 colonies of refugee children were disbanded. ... We were informed that our hospital and equipment were needed for orphan children. Therefore the sick children were removed to the Provincial Hospital to be nursed by nuns. ... We had the good fortune of meeting some of these friends again in Madrid. One mother told us how it had taken six days and nights to get there travelling in cattle trucks. ... Her baby had died on the second day; her home was destroyed. It was very difficult [to] obtain food or work.

In April the Quaker Howard Kershner, Director of Relief for the International Commission, drove from Paris to Spain to re-assess the

Commission's work following the fall of the Republican Government. Kershner, a successful New York businessman, was also charged with coordinating all of the AFSC's relief activities.

"Early in March it became evident that Republican Spain would not endure much longer", he reported.

> Every effort was made to obtain assurances from the Burgos [Nationalist] Government that the lives of our workers, our food supplies, cars and trucks would be protected, during the period of change and after the Nationalists had extended their authority over all of Spain.
>
> During February and March, the Commission continued to send whole cargo shipments of food to Republican Spanish ports. When these ships left Marseilles, London or other ports, it was not known whether Republican Spain would last until after they had reached Valencia [where the Commission had a storehouse]. In many cases the owners of the ships and the crews felt very uncertain as to their fate should the Republic fall before the ships discharged and left Spanish ports. In several instances, both the crews and the owners refused to have the ships dock in Republican Spanish ports. In order to obviate this difficulty this Commission made strenuous representations to the Burgos Government, and not only secured specific assurances that such ships would be exempt from the blockade, but that if they arrived in Valencia after the change, the cargoes would be unloaded and left peaceably in our possession, and the ships themselves allowed to depart unmolested.

The Commission was also told that all local officials had been informed of the need to cooperate with its workers and that its supplies and property should not be interfered with. But when Nationalist troops took over southern Spain they immediately seized lorries and food supplies belonging to the Commission and closed down its food canteens in Valencia. Emmet Gulley, its representative there, was not even allowed to set foot on the docks. At this point the decision was made to send

Kershner to Valencia to discuss the situation face-to-face with Spanish officials. He later wrote:

> They assured [me] that the situation had been very difficult for a week or ten days after the fall of the Republic. Communications were so disorganized that it was almost impossible for officials in Burgos (who were also at this time engaged in moving their offices to Madrid) to communicate with the local authorities in Southern Spain. ... These cities were all under Martial Law, the army was hungry and the local commanders took everything in sight.

When Kershner arrived in Valencia he discovered that the local military commander had issued orders that the Commission's stores there, as well as supplies unloaded from two of its chartered ships, were to be turned over to the local civilian authorities and sold. Cargo from five other ships had been seized and taken to army storehouses. Vigorous representations were immediately made to General Aranda, Commander of the Department of the East.

> The general assured the Director in a very beautiful speech that the Army had taken these supplies merely to protect them until the rightful owners could be located. Now that this was known, all supplies would be returned promptly, and any missing items paid for.

When it emerged that most of the supplies had already been consumed by the army Kershner dispatched a 500-word telegram to General Franco himself, warning that without the immediate replacement of the missing stocks no further supplies would be sent to Spain. In his report, an obviously frustrated Kershner continued:

> If the reader is to understand the situation at all he must get the picture of every railway car and every lorry dashing about loaded with soldiers for parades and reviews, with the time of officials

> and the populace taken up in fiestas, bullfights and military demonstrations. Food may be spoiling within half a mile of starving people, with great numbers of lorries being used for the transport of soldiers and vast numbers of men and children of all ages marching in parades, and still not a lorry or man available with which to move food.
>
> It required one week of strenuous effort to get two special trains of 40 cars each loaded on the dock at Valencia and started to Madrid. The next day a 13-car train load was sent to Murcia, Alicante and Madrid.

Having travelled to Madrid himself, Kershner was assured by the authorities there that the missing supplies would be replaced, using the army's general stores. Despite his initial doubts about the likelihood of this happening, his threat to cut off further food supplies obviously concentrated the minds of the generals because most of the shortfall in stocks was eventually made good.

After meeting with the officials now charged with food distribution Kershner briefed Mary and each of her 30 colleagues still working in Spain on the latest situation. Of chief concern was the fact that under the new regime responsibility for running their life-saving food canteens was being taken from their hands to be henceforth organised by inexperienced local authorities. "The most our workers can do from now on is to go about, observing, inspecting, suggesting and assisting. … It is believed that these workers will be able to carry an effective message of love and friendship from the people of many countries, who have given so generously to help the people of Spain," wrote Kershner, gallantly attempting to put a positive spin on this heavy blow to Quaker relief efforts.

Fourteen workers chose to stay. Mary and the rest of her colleagues took the view that, deprived of an active role in Spain, the time had come to continue their work elsewhere. Kershner's report continued: "It ordinarily requires two to three months to get permission to leave Spain, but in view of the splendid work which these people had done permission was granted immediately."

On 5 May 1939, their hearts heavy with foreboding for the future of the children they were being forced to abandon, Mary and a number of her colleagues reluctantly drove across the border into France with Kershner, taking with them all the records of their work in Spain. "But always with the idea that I'd get back to work with the Spaniards", she later recalled. Less than three months later Mary made good on these words when she returned to the beaches of Roussillon to try to bring some relief to the thousands of refugees languishing in the squalid internment camps.

The Quakers were not the only group to be made unwelcome in Franco's Spain. Less than a fortnight later the Swiss SCI volunteers were ordered out of the country by government directive. The new regime had greater concerns than the fate of sick women and children, especially those it deemed to be 'reds'.

***

After crossing into France with Howard Kershner, Mary made her way to London before travelling back to Cork for what must have been an emotional reunion with her widowed mother and her brother. Yet, the suffering and death she had witnessed in Spain and the ongoing plight in France of those she considered "my Spanish friends" was never far from her thoughts. In early July 1939 she was interviewed by the International Commission for Child Refugees and immediately offered a position in a small internment camp for women.

In fact, Mary never actually took up this position in the women's camp because when Dorothy Morris, who was by now working among the Spanish refugees along the French coast, heard that her Irish friend was in France she arranged for them to work together again – this time in the camp at Barcarès. In a letter written in August 1939 to her family in New Zealand, quoted by Mark Derby, Dorothy Morris wrote:

> I had too much work to manage alone, so my great friend and fellow worker of my Spanish days has been sent out to work here too … she only left in May … I think I may have mentioned her

> name, Mary Elmes. … We have an enormous correspondence with the camps; and Mary has beautiful Spanish and French, but it has grown to such an extent, and the requests are so varied, that we are about to engage a Spanish secretary, since M was spending all her days madly typing.

On July 14 Mary wrote to the Spain Committee in Friends House that she was being put in charge of cultural activities of the camps. This work, crucial for raising the morale of the inmates and alleviating the tedium of camp existence, involved setting up classes for children and adults as well as supplying books, musical instruments and artists' materials.

> I think that the work will be most interesting and I hope that the years that I spent at college in the study of Spanish literature will prove of something more than the purely personal pleasure that they have been so far and be useful now in the choosing of books for the libraries that it is proposed to start for the men. … Thank you very much for getting me back into this work again. I cannot tell you how glad I am to have the prospect of doing something for my Spanish friends again.

Despite her glittering academic achievements Mary had chosen to turn her back on a conventional career and was once again on her way to support desperate people struggling to survive in dire conditions. But as she made her way through France to the squalid refugee camps in the shadow of the Pyrenees she could never have imagined that the path she had chosen would ultimately lead her into the deadly heart of the Holocaust and deliver her into the hands of the Gestapo.

***

By the time Mary arrived on the Roussillon coast the situation in the camps had stabilised to some extent – initially largely due to the efforts of the inmates themselves. The French authorities had provided the tools and materials while the Spaniards had provided the manpower. Within a few weeks the men had built a series of barracks. The structures mainly consisted of long, wooden walls, topped by a pitched roof of timber spars which was covered in canvas sheeting. Although basic, these bare wooden barracks must have seemed like a luxury to refugees who had endured weeks of living on bare sand, exposed to wind and rain.

Although Mary's primary focus was on cultural activities for the refugees, she quickly identified a more pressing need outside her official remit and set up a milk distribution service for the 2,000 severely malnourished young children and elderly camp inmates. On this project she worked in conjunction with Elisabeth Eidenbenz, a Swiss teacher who had founded a maternity hospital in a run-down chateau near the village of Elne to provide care for pregnant women from the camps and their newborn infants. Like Mary, Elisabeth Eidenbenz had volunteered for aid work in Spain. When she followed the refugees into France she was appalled by the lack of facilities for pregnant women in the camps and the high rates of infant mortality, and decided to establish a maternity hospital herself. Just outside the nearby village at Elne she found a roofless, run-down chateau. Using local labour and a grant from Aide Suisse aux Enfants, Elisabeth had the building renovated and opened her hospital in November 1939. Mary's main role was to organise permission for pregnant refugees to leave the camps to attend the maternity hospital. Until its closure in 1944 by the Gestapo almost 600 children were born in La Maternité d'Elne, safely removed from the disease-ridden squalor of the camps.

In a move designed to improve the situation for new mothers and their babies returning to Argelès from the hospital at Elne, the International Commission persuaded the camp authorities to convert one of the barracks into a crèche where mothers and babies could live and be given supplementary food. The crèche opened in February 1940 after the Commission agreed to cover the cost of supplying extra flooring, furnishing and heating, and the construction of a kitchen.

"The low average weight of all babies born in Elne in December January had indicated the necessity for this", reads one AFSC report, which goes on to point out that there was insufficient accommodation in the Maternité at Elne for this extra number of women.

> Extra nourishment is given, consisting of fresh milk and cocoa, fresh fruit, vegetables, cod-liver oil, etc. The direction is shared by an Aide Swiss nurse and a Spanish doctor working under the French authority. The Commission provides all supplies.

On the cultural front Mary worked closely with Francisco Pons, one of the Spanish inmates, to establish in the camp a school for children, soon followed by a library for adults.

In memoirs or interviews, acquaintances of Mary frequently refer to her moral presence and her quiet, but steely, assertiveness. She combined these traits with an easy personal charm that could persuade even hidebound bureaucrats to relax the rules for her or look the other way when her ambitions exceeded her official role. In the camp at Argelès, for example, she prevailed upon the camp commander to sanction the building of a separate barracks for fourteen- to seventeen-year-old boys. With so many inmates from all walks of life, possessing a vast range of skills, Mary's projects cost the authorities very little to put into practice yet immeasurably improved the situation inside the camps. This barracks served as both living quarters and a schoolroom for the teenagers. Lessons were provided by teachers among those being held in the camp.

An AFSC report on cultural work in September 1939 highlighted the improved conditions:

> Now they live in wooden huts built by the French authorities and have sufficient food, although many suffer from rheumatism and chest infections due to their former sufferings and through having to sleep on the bare ground. Most of them look fairly healthy. Their mental sufferings are as great as ever. They are absolutely without occupation and see little hope of making new lives for themselves.

In order to combat this state of affairs Mary and her colleagues began setting up schools in each of the camps, giving classes in a wide variety of subjects with professional teachers and inmates with technical knowledge:

> … who are those helping themselves to forget despair and lifting their comrades out of inertia and boredom.
>
> Since only small quantities of school materials are occasionally given by the French authorities, the real work of supplying the most essential stationery was begun with a grant of £80 given by the London and Birmingham Quakers. This amount was largely spent on suppliers of school materials and books for the camps at Argelès, St Cyprien, Barcarès and Vernet.

In July the International Commission made a grant of £500 for the scheme.

> Out of that sum and in collaboration with the French military authorities of the camp who supplied the building, a central library and reading room for general readers, with 1,500 text books and novels in Spanish has been opened in the camp of Barcarès and a small collection of textbooks for the exclusive use of the teachers has been sent to the central commission of culture in the same camp. Barcarès is the largest of the refugee camps and has from 80,000 to 100,000 men.

The wooden building which served as the reading room was of basic construction similar to the barracks in which the men lived, with sloping walls and an unboarded floor. One section was reserved for the librarian and his staff and the remainder furnished with wooden tables and benches.

> The bookcases have been painted bright blue and the carpenters have made one or two pieces of modern furniture to give an air of civilisation to the otherwise rather rough interior. A cactus plant in a pot has even been produced from somewhere.

Originally the building was designed to accommodate 150 readers but it proved so popular that within a week it could not accommodate the numbers turning up looking for books and had to be enlarged to twice its previous size to accommodate the overflow of readers who were forced to sit on the sand and anywhere else they could find room.

> The amount of room is still pitifully inadequate and the readers queue up, often for two hours before the doors open, so as to be sure of securing a seat and obtaining the book they are reading. …
>
> There are twenty-seven little boys between the ages of six and sixteen at Barcarès and we have supplied their school with stationery, maps, geometrical instruments, etc. and have recently given them a small library of some 100 textbooks and adventure stories.

Soon the adult schools had enough supplies of stationery for 10,000 students. The camp population was divided into groups of 2,000, each of which had its own school equipped with a supply of French and English grammars for language classes. An AFSC report noted that:

> The central hospital at Barcarès, where thirty Spanish doctors, pharmacists and male nurses work under the direction of the French chief, has been sent a collection of general literature and French grammars and dictionaries and also some second-hand medical works in Spanish and French. We are continuing to look for other medical texts in an attempt to fill to some extent the long list they sent eagerly to us when we intimated that we would try to supply a small medical library.

The camp at Agde housed around 10,000 Catalans. When the AFSC presented them with a gift of 350 books in their language, the French authorities responded by building a reading room which was duly opened on 11 September, the Catalan national festival. Such was the interest generated by the library scheme that the AFSC even received an appeal for books from a French internment camp in Algeria:

> Our correspondent says that the French authorities are friendly to the idea of a library and have placed a barrack at the disposal of the men to serve as the reading room. We hope that in spite of the difficulties of transport we shall be able to send some small quantities of books to lighten the tedium of this camp where the physical and moral conditions are much more unendurable even than those in the south of France.

The most sought-after books were French grammars and dictionaries:

> Practically every refugee is anxious to learn French so as to be better equipped and more useful when he eventually leaves the camp and we feel that by facilitating individual study to supplement classwork we are helping to attain this very desirable end. …
>
> The greatest desire of these refugees is to inform themselves of recent developments in their trade or profession and so recover some of the ground lost during three years of war and eight months spent in a concentration camp.

One exotic request came from the teacher of a group of silkworm industry workers. These men had been accepted by a South American republic as immigrants suitable to develop the local silkworm industry. The men all had considerable hands-on experience of their trade but were keen to study the more technical side of their trade, so they asked the AFSC to attempt to procure a specific textbook for them. Miraculously, it arrived one day in the camp.

> When their teacher acknowledged it he said the men are greatly encouraged by the gift of this book and feel that their new life has begun already. Similar phrases occur in nearly all of the letters of acknowledgement that we receive. There are constant references

> to new courage and hope received from books we have sent and from the knowledge that although the recipients are shut away from civilisation they are not completely forgotten by the rest of the world.

In May 1940 Margaret Frawley, an American journalist and Quaker, drew up a report for the AFSC on the enthusiasm displayed by the Republicans in the camps for ways to improve their situation through study and keeping their minds occupied. Such was the men's determination to break the curse of boredom that when Mary brought the first books to the camps the men queued for hours to borrow from the small libraries.

> It was natural, therefore, that when they went out into work companies they no sooner had a post office address before they had a study club going and were asking for books. The most popular clubs are, of course, those where the men can learn French. …
>
> The man who has most information takes the book, if there is only one, and the class. There are classes in English, advanced mathematics, applied mathematics, electricity, mechanical assemblage and construction, and a dozen other fields.
>
> Mary, the Commission worker, who is in direct charge of this program and who has had a voluminous correspondence with the Spanish workers, establishes the study libraries only with the consent of the French commandant of each company. She has one simple rule in selecting books: 'Nothing religious, nothing political or contentious.'

As ever, Mary was scrupulous in making sure all the workers benefitted equally from the progamme, regardless of their social position or educational background and is quoted in the report as stating that:

> Our chief interest so far has not been solely in intellectuals. I feel that the Commission can do a great deal more by concentrating rather on groups of men whose cultural opportunities have never

> been very great or perhaps even have been nil, rather than on a very much smaller group of intellectuals who, although they are deprived of the intellectual activities to which they have been accustomed, have, in their time, enjoyed very great opportunities, and are always better equipped to make the most of an occasion which may be presented to them in the future.
>
> The most interesting part of the struggle in Spain was that it was directly identified with the raising of the level of culture for those who were not able to attend universities and health professions and it seems worthwhile to try to carry on the tradition.
>
> Because of the difficulty of obtaining many books in Europe now, there are many gaps in the present collections which American groups might be willing to help fill. …
>
> In the face of widespread needs for food and clothing, this appeal for books may seem less important than other demands. It is an appeal for men who have kept their morale, who have met adversity with courage and resourcefulness, and who are helping themselves. They ask only [for] the tools.

As Mary was well aware, the refugees responded eagerly to any opportunity that allowed them to improve their situation. Accordingly, when a set of carpenter's tools and a supply of paint were sent into the camp as a gift, the refugees set up a small workshop to make educational toys which they supplied to the children's schools at Argelès and elsewhere.

Also with children in mind, Mary organised the construction of five other barracks in Argelès for those up to the fourteen years of age. These buildings, which were located close to the women's accommodation so that mothers could keep an eye on their children, served as centres for study and various creative activities. The final strand of Mary's plans for the camp's children involved building a school for three- to five-year-olds. It was soon catering for 500 pupils. Quaker funding enabled Mary to supply desks, blackboards, copybooks and most other requirements of a normal school.

Francisco Pons, Mary's 'librarian', quickly found himself overseeing a two-room building housing 3,000 volumes in Spanish, French and

English. In his memoirs he recalled how one afternoon an ebullient 'Miss Mary', as she was known to the inmates, excitedly swept through the camp gates in a car crammed with books and musical instruments. Today, in her home near Perpignan, Mary's daughter Caroline proudly displays small animals carved from bone – painstakingly fashioned by grateful inmates as gifts for a woman who worked unstintingly to improve their lives.

Although strictly outside her job description, Mary also played a vital role in reuniting anguished families who had been split up by the French authorities.

"I had a small office in the camp", she remembered. "Women would come in to me asking me to find their husband, who might be in another camp." This role of re-uniting families torn apart by war or internment would become a constant in the work Mary carried out in the camps. As late as the summer of 1942, as the convoys to the death camps rumbled eastwards, she faced a barrage of frantic appeals from people desperately trying to locate loved ones before they were boarded onto the trains.

***

The scale of relief brought to southwest France by the AFSC undoubtedly saved countless lives. In his 1941 report, AFSC worker Gilbert White records that 'Les Quakers Americain' were feeding 7,200 adult refugees and 800 children daily in camps and hospitals. In addition, 500 children were being looked after full-time in children's colonies. A further 2,000 children were being provided with supplemental food in the form of milk and vitamins. More than 200 children were being fed in their own homes and 3,100 French children were provided with a meal at school.

The aid provided by the AFSC extended beyond supplying food to the starving: "Over the course of the year, 1,500 people had been interviewed and given assistance with emigration. One hundred refugee workers had been supported in small ateliers and more than Fr.1 million, sent by the British Friends Service Council, had been distributed to 550 refugees."

By 1942, diseases such as TB were becoming prevalent, and there was high mortality among the elderly and infirm. The standard French ration card provided for only 1,000 calories a day and malnourishment was common both inside and outside the camps.

"Children often fainted at school and stomachs distended from malnutrition were becoming a common sight. Clothing too is scarce. Children were coming to school barefoot", the report continued. One of the Quaker-run ateliers provided espadrilles, which, as Gilbert noted, "provided little warmth but at least kept feet off the ground." In the camps of Gurs and Rivesaltes the food provided was no longer enough to sustain life. The vast majority of those in the camps were now Jewish and mass deportations to the death camps had begun. The Quakers and the other aid agencies working in the camps were unanimous as to what needed to be done: at all costs the children had to be saved.

Mary and her mother, Elisabeth.

Mary and her father, Edward.

Mary and John as children.

Mary as a child.

Mary as a teenager at home in Cork.

Studio photo of Mary taken before she went to Spain.

Mary's graduation from Trinity; Mary second from left in front row.

Trinity College Dublin.

Ambulance driver Juan, Mary and Dorothy Morris in Spain.

Mary (in gloves) manning food station in Spain.

Food station, Spain; Mary on left, Howard Kerchner on the right.

Feeding the children in a camp in Spain, unknown woman.

Children eating in camp in Spain.

Mary and the injured infant Palmira Sanchez.

Portrait of Mary in her AFSC uniform by Balbino Giner.

AFSC delegates making up food packages, unknown location.

Mary napping in the sunshine.

AFSC delegates; Mary in front row, sixth from the left.

Secours Quakers loading up supplies in France.

Argelès camp on the beach.

3

In Flight from Hitler

In 1933, shortly after attaining power in Germany, Nazi leaders set about carrying out their pledge to persecute Jews by excluding them from all aspects of 'Aryan' society and stripping them of their civil and legal rights. In April a decree was issued curtailing the rights of Jewish doctors to practise their profession. In Berlin, Dr Eva Freund suddenly found herself deprived of her chosen livelihood. That same year Eva and her husband Hans, a consultant engineer, made the decision to leave their home in Germany and relocate to Milan, where their first son, Mario, was born three years later. In 1938 the family moved to Paris where Hans worked for the state railway company, SNCF.

The Freunds formed part of a steady flow of Jews from Germany and Eastern Europe towards the west, a trend that had begun in the aftermath of the First World War and became a flood after the Nazi Party rose to power. As the country where the rights of man were enshrined in its Constitution, France was a natural choice for those seeking sanctuary. Initially the French proved to be willing hosts to these new arrivals. However, the ongoing aftershock of the Great Depression, coupled with the unstable political situation in Europe, led many countries to re-examine their policies towards immigrants. As the decade advanced, France saw an increase in anti-Semitic sentiments, fuelled by the right-wing press and other extreme elements.

As Hitler's territorial ambitions became apparent, German Jewish refugees were joined by those from Austria and Czechoslovakia. The Nazi Anschluss of Austria in March 1938 gave way on 9–10 November to 'Kristallnacht' in Germany – so-named because of the broken glass that littered the streets when Jews and their property were attacked by brown-shirted thugs – accelerating the flow of Jews fleeing west. In France this trend played into the hands of the anti-Semites who had been fomenting hatred of Jews for decades. In response to this growing antipathy among the French public towards immigrants, the government of the Third Republic began to impose restrictions on immigration. In 1938 it passed a law giving regional governors, known as prefects, authority to construct internment camps to hold 'undesirable aliens'.

In June 1940 the number of foreign and stateless Jewish refugees in France stood at 180,000, with thousands being held in internment camps around the country, together with numerous non-Jewish opponents of the Nazis. By far the largest number of refugees were held in the south and southwest, where Mary and her colleagues were based, but many others were interned in the northern part of the country. On 3 September 1939 Hans Freund was arrested under the 1938 law and interned at Villerbon, near Blois, a hillside village overlooking the River Loire to the southwest of Paris. Eva, heavily pregnant with their second child, was left behind with her young son.

On 10 May 1940 Hitler abruptly signalled the end of the Phoney War, which had seen an eight-month hiatus in military operations on the Western Front, by launching a Blitzkreig attack on the Low Countries, sparking the flight into France of thousands more refugees. Stunned French military chiefs watched in horrified disbelief as enemy forces rapidly sidestepped their much-vaunted defensive Maginot Line and rumbled unopposed into France. Even the German High Command was surprised by the speed of its advance and the lack of meaningful resistance by French troops. As early as 15 May a dejected French Prime Minister Paul Reynaud telephoned his British counterpart Winston Churchill to inform him that he believed the Battle of France had already been lost. On 28 May Belgium conceded defeat and capitulated. By the middle of June the German vanguard had reached the outskirts of Paris, just days behind the retreating French Army. As military and government leaders struggled to respond to these latest developments panic took hold among those living in the City of Light, prompting an exodus to the south by millions of its citizens. On 10 June the Government – riven by dissent over whether to continue the war or sign an armistice with Hitler – made the decision to leave the city, initially transferring to Touraine in the Loire Valley. Fearful of being overtaken by the invading forces, French officials pressed on to Bordeaux on the Atlantic coast, finally installing themselves in the spa town of Vichy. Before leaving the capital, officials at the Ministry of Foreign Affairs had ordered staff to burn thousands of state dossiers. To the fleeing Parisians the massive black pall drifting skywards over the Left Bank from the ministry courtyards must have appeared as a sombre omen, presaging a return to the Dark Ages.

Ireland's Paris-based diplomats, anticipating the need to evacuate their offices in the 16th arrondissement, had rented a villa in Septeuil, a village 50 kilometres southwest of the capital. In the event, however, the two senior diplomats, Con Cremin and Seán Murphy – who would play a major role when Mary Elmes was arrested – never availed of this villa and left Paris on the same day as the French Government, deeming it more prudent to find premises closer to the Spanish border.

Many people chose trains to escape but in the pandemonium stations were quickly overwhelmed by the volume of people mobbing the ticket desks. Thousands of would-be passengers gathered outside stations, only for many to find that after a fruitless hours-long wait their only option was to sleep in the streets when the last overcrowded trains of the evening departed without them. The *Sunday Times* Paris correspondent, Virginia Cowles, reported on 16 June 1940:

> Many thousands of people with bundles and bags were on the streets begging to be let into the station. The police were holding them back, telling them that there were no more trains leaving Paris.
>
> Paris was a tragic sight. The sun streamed through the chestnut trees, but gone were the laughing crowds along the boulevards, the rich smell of tobacco, and there were no splashing fountains and noisy cabs. Only a sweep of deserted streets.

The report goes on to hint at the scale of demoralisation among the military. "Several times when we were crossing the main squares we saw groups of soldiers, their faces black with dust and full marching kit on their backs, limping warily along; evidently they were back from the front, but there was nobody to cheer them."

The roads south and west of the city quickly became gridlocked by the sea of civilians and sundry vehicles. Cowles' report continues: "As we drove down the Seine I thought I had never seen Paris looking more beautiful. For ten hours we averaged four miles an hour. The exodus had to be seen to be believed – an unbroken flow of human beings bicycling, riding and trudging along the roads." An estimated four million Parisians – four-fifths of the city's population – took part in the exodus. Most of those who remained mainly lived in poorer areas of the city and could not afford to flee. Others were people who for various reasons simply had to stay. Cowles reported how the concierge of the *Sunday Times* office had chosen to stay out of defiance, saying "his father had lived through the Prussian invasion in 1870, he had lived through 1914 and now his family would have to live through 1940. 'It will not last', he said. 'They have come before and they have left before.'"

The French Government had made preparations ahead of the arrival in May of the earlier wave of refugees fleeing the Low Countries and Alsace-Lorraine ahead of the Germans, and most of these had been organised into groups and dispersed to the various internment camps by the SNCF. No such plan had been put in place for the evacuation of Paris, possibly for fear of demoralising its inhabitants by implying that France would fall to Hitler's forces. Not unexpectedly, the exodus quickly degenerated into chaos.

One eyewitness, quoted in *Fleeing Hitler*, by Hanna Diamond, described the scene he encountered as he tried to make his way out of the city:

> There were lorries, cars, bicycles, horses, perambulators and wheelbarrows all mixed up with pedestrians of every age, type, size and description. Some of the cars were straight from the showroom; others looked as if they had been rescued from refuse dumps. And every vehicle was laden to capacity with anything you can think of, from an empty parrot cage to a grandfather

clock. The desire to save as much as possible from the invader was later to spell tragedy for many, and from the next day onwards we were to see hundreds and hundreds of cars with smashed axles lying by the roadside – while their owners either trudged on with what they could carry or helplessly waited for assistance that never came.

Most travellers had to rely on whatever food they had taken with them because earlier waves of the exodus had exhausted supplies in towns and villages along the way. Fortunately the weather was warm and dry so those on the road were spared the freezing nightmare endured by the Republicans who had struggled over the Pyrenees in the winter of 1939. In fact, the weather that fateful summer was exceptionally hot, a boon to the throngs who found hotels and *pensions* along their route full to capacity, forcing them to sleep in barns, outbuildings or open fields. Along the way, the refugees encountered retreating French military convoys, whose presence among them, many civilians feared, would invite attacks by the Luftwaffe. A number of air raids against the fleeing civilians had indeed taken place and remained a constant fear among those on the roads.

As Hanna Diamond has pointed out, the fleeing French were now effectively refugees in their own country. For the large numbers of Jews from all over Europe who found themselves in Paris the flight from the capital held a bitter poignancy. All had sought sanctuary in France and now found themselves fleeing the Nazis once more. With the news that the capital had been declared an 'open city' – meaning it would not offer any resistance to the invaders and would therefore not be attacked – many of those heading south would return to their homes over the coming weeks. For Jews fleeing for their lives, however, the possibility of returning to Paris was but a distant hope. For thousands more Jews this hoped-for return would never materialise as shamefully, and tragically, almost 80,000 of them – whether foreign-born or French – would be hunted down and sent from France to their deaths in the East.

***

The speed of France's catastrophic defeat alarmed the International Commission, which urgently instructed its British and Commonwealth members working in France to escape to Britain by ship for fear the whole country would soon be under German occupation. Once again the New Zealander Dorothy Morris faced the heartbreak of having to abandon desolate people to whom she had devoted such care. And once again, despite the dangers, Mary Elmes chose to remain in France with the refugees in the camps, relying for her personal safety on the fact that she was a citizen of a neutral country – a protection enshrined in international law but one she must have suspected might be contemptuously dismissed by the Nazis occupiers, as indeed it was. Mary and her colleagues knew from firsthand experience in Spain that the Luftwaffe had honed its deadly skills by attacking civilians and were not surprised to hear reports of air attacks on the terrified masses snaking their way south. With the public transport system overwhelmed and the country in chaos, Mary offered to drive Dorothy and her other colleagues from Perpignan to Bordeaux, setting off on 17 June, three days after German troops marched into Paris. In a desperate bid to reach the port city before the Germans cut off their escape route, the party set off on the 400-kilometre journey after sunset to lessen the risk of an air attack. As Mark Derby recounts:

> Their car reached Bordeaux in the early dawn of mid-summer, finding it a wretched city, over-run with fugitives from throughout Western Europe, many of them sleeping on the streets and all seemingly frantic to obtain travel permits, fares and tickets to a safe destination. At the International Commission office on the rue Vergniaud, these documents were provided by the anxious and assiduous Margaret Frawley, who told the carload of tussled and weary evacuees that they immediately needed to drive on to the coastal port of Le Verdon, where the ship was waiting to leave. The scream of the dive bomber, defending ack-ack fire and the boom of explosives accompanied them on this final stage of the journey, through miles of vineyards bearing the names of famous vintages.

> The road followed the course of the River Garonne to a wide estuary where it discharged into the Atlantic. Some distance offshore a muddy-yellow liner lay at anchor, and her launch shuttled to and fro throughout the morning to ferry passengers aboard. On a quay littered with cars abandoned by their departing owners, Dorothy and Mary bid each other a tearful farewell. They had worked closely and harmoniously together for more than three years, sometimes in conditions of great hardship and personal risk, but also in circumstances that both of them were afterwards happy to recall.

The ship that Dorothy and her colleagues were crammed aboard was the SS *Madura*, an ageing cargo vessel that plied the routes between Britain and the Far East and had been on its way back from India when it was ordered by Churchill to divert to Bordeaux to rescue trapped civilians. Daphne Wall was just a child when she and her British parents arrived in Bordeaux to join the more than one million other refugees cramming into the city. As the *Madura* prepared to set sail that evening she was lying well below her Plimsoll line (the line on its hull indicating the vessel's maximum safe draft): nervous passengers expecting air raids had been boarding the ship for the previous twenty-four hours and somehow 1,500 refugees had struggled aboard – nearly ten times more than the Madura was designed to carry.

"Every square inch of deck was covered with sleeping bodies wrapped in coats and blankets," Daphne recalled in her book, *The World I Lost*. "They looked more like ghostly corpses in the half-light, though some of them were beginning to stir and pour cups of tea out of thermos flasks." Despite her battered appearance, the *Madura*'s passenger list featured some notable names, among them Baron Rothschild and Marie Curie's daughter Eve. A group of British foreign correspondents, including novelist Graham Greene's brother Hugh, who had been reporting from Paris for the *Daily Telegraph*, had also made their way on board. The journalists, defiantly ebullient despite the threat of imminent air attack and the fact that the ship would be traveling without the benefit of a naval escort, boarded the *Madura* with an impressive collection of local vintages and installed themselves in a corner of the deck, determined to party their way home.

As a trained nurse, Dorothy Morris would have introduced herself to the ship's Irish surgeon, Thomas Kelly, in case her services were required during the voyage. Kelly, a 69-year-old staunch Catholic from County Galway, had had an extraordinary military career as an army doctor and seen action in countless conflicts, including two world wars. At the outbreak of the Second World War he gamely tried to enlist in the Royal Navy but was rejected because of his age. Bitterly disappointed but determined to play some part in the conflict, he joined the British Merchant Navy. After the evacuation of Bordeaux, Kelly accompanied the Eighth Army to Egypt before serving on Atlantic convoys. His lengthy career came to a close in 1944 when he was finally forced to retire shortly after serving aboard troopships transporting soldiers for the D-Day invasion of Europe.

As evening settled over Bordeaux the over-crowded old freighter slipped its moorings and heaved itself out into the open sea. The hubbub from its packed decks gradually died away over the grey water as Mary followed the *Madura*'s slow progress until old ship faded from sight.

Standing alone on the now eerily deserted quay, Mary's heart must have been heavy with a mixture of sadness at her friends' departure and foreboding for the future, now that real war had finally come to France. Twilight was giving way to darkness as she made her way along the pier, alert for the drone of the bombers that would attack the city in earnest the following night. Among the rows of deserted cars she located her own and with one last glance over the ocean set off for home through the silent vineyards.

***

In the years following the First World War France had welcomed immigrants to take the place of workers killed in the conflict. Thousands of Jews, mainly from Eastern Europe, made their way to France, the traditional European haven for refugees. But as the continent drifted ever closer to all-out war, the Government of the Third Republic began to reassess its policies on new arrivals. On 12 November 1938, amid a crisis of national identity and rising xenophobia as a seemingly endless stream of fugitives from Nazism sought refuge in France, the Government passed a decree allowing for the internment of 'undesirable aliens', a category that was liberally interpreted and came to include Jews, communists and Freemasons. The names of the camps constructed to hold these people live on in infamy to evoke memories of the darkest period of modern French history: Gurs, Rivesaltes, Noé, Récebédou, Vernet, Argelès, Rieucros, Saint Cyprien – a shameful network of what came to be known as 'les camps de mépris' – the camps of scorn.

On 16 June 1940, two days after the first German troops marched triumphantly into Paris, Prime Minister Paul Reynaud resigned. The following day, Marshal Phillipe Pétain, an aging hero of the First World War Battle of Verdun, was made President of the Council of Ministers and immediately requested an armistice, which was signed on 22 June and came into effect three days later. As part of its terms France was divided into two distinct zones: an Occupied Zone administered by the Nazis, comprising the north of the country including Bordeaux and the Atlantic coast, and a so-called Free Zone in the south and southwest governed by Pétain's Vichy Government. Article 19 of the Armistice gave the German authorities powers to extricate from either zone political refugees or other individuals wanted by the Gestapo, a move that caused widespread alarm among the thousands of 'undesirables' in the French internment camps.

On 10 July the Third Republic ceased to exist when it voted to grant full powers to Pétain by appointing him Chief of State. The republican-minded national motto since the French Revolution – *liberté, égalité, fraternité* – was no longer deemed appropriate and gave way to a slogan of *travail, famille, patrie* (labour, family, fatherland), reflecting the new regime's conservative political and social agenda. The Vichy Government lost no time in activating the xenophobic, anti-Semitic and authoritarian policies that would mark its years in power and soon see even French-born Jews treated as second-class citizens.

In all, 600,000 people would pass through 200 camps established all over the country. By December 1940, after the fall of France, 55,000 people of various races and religions were being held in camps in the southern Vichy 'Free Zone', compared to 3,000 in Nazi-occupied France.

On 22 July the government set up a committee to review the status of all French citizens who had benefitted from the introduction in 1927 of liberal laws designed to make naturalisation of Eastern European immigrants easier. In the 1920s most foreign Jews who came to France were in search of work; in the 1930s the majority were political refugees.

Established Jewish families, some of them in France for generations, considered themselves to be French first and Jewish second and felt little empathy with the later arrivals. In fact, many of the established Jews resented the presence in France of so many newcomers, whom they blamed for the prevailing mood of anti-Semitism sweeping the country.

In the face of catastrophic military defeat, the fall of the republican administration and the disintegration of the country's social and economic fabric, the priority for Pétain's regime was to divert culpability for this debacle away from the French themselves. Thus was born the pretence that the defeat was caused not by the gross incompetence of politicians and military leaders employing out-dated tactics, but by a cabal of malign outsiders who had infiltrated French society, destroying the country from within.

For French historian Denis Peschanski, the choice to collaborate with Germany was made by the French Government at the time of the Armistice in June 1940:

> Later Hitler and Pétain met in a small railway station in Provence, in Montoir on October 24, 1940 and it as if they were sealing their collaboration, a collaboration that was wanted by Vichy because for the new French government the cause of the defeat wasn't Germany's military superiority or the ineptitude of its politicians but the presence in France of Jews, communists, foreigners and Freemasons. Therefore to regenerate French society from within and to get out of the crisis it was necessary to gather together the 'pure' elements around French traditional values: work, family, homeland. And to exclude those elements regarded as having caused the defeat.

On 13 August Vichy signalled its first move to curb the rights of Jews and foreigners when it banned Freemasons from working in certain professions. Just as it had been necessary to lock up 'undesirable' elements in internment camps to cleanse society, now it was in the nation's interest to curb the activities of those deemed detrimental to France's ambition to establish its position in a new Europe ruled by Germany. In this new France tenets that had been honoured since the Revolution were abruptly cast aside while Jews and foreigners looked on helplessly as their rights were steadily eroded. On 27 August Pétain abolished penalties for those guilty of defaming Jews, under the guise of protecting the right to free speech. This move quickly led to an outpouring of anti-Semitic propaganda, openly blaming Jews for the French defeat.

Efraim Zuroff, a Nazi hunter and head of the Jerusalem office of the Simon Wiesenthal Center, notes:

> The French hoped that they could retain as much of their sovereignty as possible but in fact they became a satellite state; you could say a colony of the Germans.
>
> It started in the usual bureaucratic way of Jews being forbidden to work for the government, being designated in a certain way, marked, being deprived of their livelihood even, being taken for forced labour and in some cases being sent to camps already.
>
> These camps were set up by the Vichy Government and served the purpose of keeping these people on hold until ultimately they were sent to the death camps. They officially were sent to an 'unknown destination' … it's not clear who knew exactly what that meant. I'm sure that the amount of knowledge that existed in '42 was less than existed in '43/'44 but what was clear from the very beginning was that these people were never going to return.

On 3 October the new government passed the first in a series of overtly anti-Semitic laws, known as the Statuts des Juifs. These mirrored the anti-Jewish decrees being put in place by the German authorities in the Occupied Zone, although in time they would outdo in harshness those being decreed in occupied France by the Nazis. A second statute was promulgated in June 1941. The effect of these laws was to exclude Jews from public life, allow them to be dismissed from their jobs in the civil service and various industries and from professions such as law, medicine and education.

On 27 September 1940 the Vichy regime passed a law defining a Jew as a person of Jewish religion or having more than two Jewish grandparents. The following day a law was passed giving local prefects sweeping powers: "Foreign nationals of the Jewish race may ... be interned in special camps by a decision of the prefect of the department of their residence", adding that, alternatively, such individuals can also be subject to house arrest on the same basis.

The majority of prefects obviously took on their new roles with enthusiasm because just four months later 40,000 foreign Jews had joined the Spanish Republicans, gypsies and other 'undesirables' being held in the camps in the Unoccupied Zone. The presence of these new internees represented an added burden for Mary and her colleagues as they strove to feed, clothe and provide rudimentary medical care to the thousands of wretched internees already languishing in the camps.

In March 1941 Pétain's government established a body called the Commissariat Général aux Questions Juives (CGQJ). The new agency's chief role was to appropriate Jewish assets and property for the French state before they fell into German hands. As a result of this measure, thousands of Jews were left destitute. Foreign Jews were particularly affected. The CGQJ established its headquarters in the Hotel Algeria in Vichy. Xavier Vallat, a veteran of the First World War, a lawyer and devout Catholic who harboured a deep hatred of Freemasons and was openly anti-Semitic, was named as first Commissioner for Jewish Affairs at the CGDJ. Jews, he believed, were "invariably dangerous". Despite his extremist views, Vallat was perceived by the Vichy government as being too lenient. In May 1942 Vallat was replaced by the odious Louis Darquier de Pellepoix, an enthusiastic Nazi collaborator and self-proclaimed anti-Semite who expressed the view that Jews should either be expelled from France or else exterminated en masse. Darquier took to his new role with relish, enriching himself in the process at the expense of the Jews he persecuted. Working in conjunction with the

Nazi occupiers he so admired, he accelerated the pace of confiscations of Jewish property in Paris and played a key role in sending thousands of Jewish children to their deaths in the extermination camps. In 1944 he was removed from his post when the German authorities uncovered the level of his corruption and inefficiency. After the war Darquier fled to Spain where he lived until his death in 1980. He was never brought to justice. In 1978 a French reporter tracked him down at his home in Spain. True to form, Darquier denied any wrongdoing and refused to accept that the Holocaust had ever taken place.

4

Rivesaltes

On a barren, wind-blown plain in the foothills of the Corbière mountains in southwest France the spectral remains of a crumbling concentration camp stand in silent rebuke. Here, at the site of the former military barracks of Camp Joffre near the rural village of Rivesaltes, people innocent of any crime were deprived of liberty and dignity and forced to live in abject squalor and starvation before being handed on to their destruction. It was here in the summer of 1942 that the camp served as the assembly centre for the thousands of Jews arrested in France's southern Unoccupied Zone. After being held for months in conditions of the utmost deprivation and despair, they were herded aboard overcrowded train carriages originally built to transport animals and delivered into the hands of their murderers. In the space of two months more than 2,289 Jewish men, women and children were deported from the camp to the gas chambers in the east by French police. Not one single German soldier was involved in this operation. France, the first European country to recognise Jews as equal before the law, had become the only country from which Germany deported Jews from territory it did not occupy. From the nearby railway station in the village of Rivesaltes the trains trundled north to the transit camp of Drancy in the suburbs of Paris, before continuing the journey eastward.

The tumbledown barracks, in the Languedoc-Roussillon wine region, cover 625 hectares (2.3 square miles) on a treeless plain covered in scrubland. In structure the camps consisted of fourteen blocks or îlots, comprising 150 barracks, each designed to accommodate seventy internees. The buildings were constructed from flimsy materials of poor quality. Rain leaked through the thin roof tiles while the wind hurtled through cracks in the walls and woodwork.

In the distance rise the mighty Pyrenees, dominated by the peak of Canigou, a mountain revered in Catalan lore. The camp, officially named Camp Joffre but more usually referred to as Rivesaltes, was built in 1938 as a military barracks to house troops in transit. On this barren plain the weather is inhospitable all year round: in winter the site is prey to freezing rain and storms; in summer a stifling heat engulfs the area and the mosquito-ridden swamps that surround it. From the north the Tramontane wind sweeps the stony plain, often blowing for weeks on end. So hostile is the climate here that a plan to construct the barracks in 1875 was abandoned when military chiefs ruled out the location as being unsuitable for cavalry horses. Yet in 1940 this very place was deemed appropriate to hold thousands of refugees from tyranny who had followed one another in wave after forlorn wave seeking safe haven in France.

The possibility of using Camp Joffre to intern the throngs of refugees in the department was first mooted in November 1940 in a memo by a Vichy official:

> The question of civilian internment camps could be dealt with easily enough if it was possible to group most of the foreign refugees together in a single camp. However, this camp [already] exists, that of Rivesaltes … which belongs to the military authorities and at the moment is only housing a few colonial troops.

Within days this suggestion was adopted and the decision made to extend the camp structure. In December 1940, much to the astonishment of the local winegrowers tending to their vines, a work party of sixty internees arrived at the camp to begin work on the new buildings.

In the first week of the new year all work was brought to a halt when a hurricane ripped through the camp. In an incident that would be repeated again and again, some barracks had tiles torn from their roofs and walls blown down, giving the refugees their first foretaste of the inclement weather that prevails on this sterile plain. The camp commandant, Captain David Gustave Humbert – a man with whom Mary would establish a close working relationship that would directly enable her to save numerous children from the convoys – sought to delay the opening of the camp until the damaged barracks could be fully repaired but was overruled by his superiors, who were anxious to transfer refugees from the camps along the coast.

Despite the stated aim of being a family residential centre, only gypsy families were allowed to stay together. All other women and children were installed in one barracks while men and boys over sixteen were placed in another. When this arrangement was queried by a visiting local official representing the Interior Minister, Captain Humbert assured him that members of the same family could see each other freely but could not eat together, at least not until the camp had been built up further.

The camp's first internees were Spanish Republicans, plucked from the overflowing internment camps of Languedoc-Roussillon to work on its construction as unpaid labourers, effectively constructing their own prison. Soon they were joined by those labelled 'undesirables': gypsies, communists and stateless refugees from Eastern and Central Europe, among them thousands of fugitive Jews.

Over the years of its existence Rivesaltes operated under a number of titles, its first being that a 'Family Residential Centre' for the mainly Spanish refugees transferred from the camps along the coast. Large numbers of Spanish men from these camps had already been co-opted into Compagnies de Travailleurs Étrangers – labour units of foreign workers which were run by the French military – to carry out work in the region.

News that the refugees were being moved to Rivesaltes was welcomed by Mary, as she explained on 6 January 1941 in a letter to Howard Kershner:

> As in other places the weather here has been exceptionally severe since the new year. There was such a strong wind and sand storms in Argelès on Saturday that six barracks in the women's camp collapsed. Part of the new sewing workshop was also blown down

> and will take about a week to re-erect. Fortunately, there was no loss of life but the women and children left 'homeless' have had to be accommodated in the school buildings and so the schools are also temporarily disjointed.
>
> There are increasing signs that the French authorities are becoming more and more concerned about the dreadful conditions in Argelès .... During an afternoon that I spent recently at the house of the prefect, he questioned me about the camp and seemed to be deeply concerned about the women and children. The French are greatly hampered on every side at the moment and there is such a lack of materials of all kinds that there seems little they can do. There is however the desire to change the refugees from Argelès to Rivesaltes. ... This move would bring a great improvement in the life of the refugees. The barracks are solidly built and new and although the camp is situated on a rather desolate, windswept plain it would not be any worse from a climatic point of view than Argelès.

Mary had been alerted to the possibility of the refugees being transferred to the camp at Rivesaltes by Helga Holbek, the Quaker delegate in Toulouse. Officials from the Interior Ministry, Helga's letter explained, were planning to use the military camp to house refugee families. The intention was to create at Rivesaltes a model camp that would ensure refugee families could remain together. Men would live in separate dormitories to women and children, with each dormitory being supervised by a trained nurse. An infirmary would also be provided. To Mary, who spent much of her time trying to re-unite families who had been scattered around the camps in the regions, this new arrangement must have appeared encouraging. Her counterparts in the other aid agencies took a more dubious line. Helga herself was sceptical of the plan and wrote to Mary: "This all sounds very beautiful; however, snag No. 1 is that it, in the best of cases, will take a long time; No. 2 is that he [the ministry official] thought there were only about 2,000 children in all the camps when the actual figure seems to be between 4,000 and 5,000."

By March, another letter from Helga to Mary made it clear that a recent meeting of the Nimes Committee* had provoked a difference of opinion among delegates. Many aid workers were reluctant to work in the new camp without the guarantee of a permanent office and preferred to hold back until conditions in the camp were improved. Helga's chief concern seems to have been that the presence of a permanent Quaker delegation in the camp would imply tacit support for the current arrangements.

Mary's vast experience in the camps had given her a sharp insight into the reality facing those being held there. In her view a boycott of the camp would impact negatively on the internees, particularly the children. As ever, Mary favoured tact over confrontation. On 14 February, Mary shared her views on the situation with Howard Kershner:

> The view of the Commission … appears to be that no collaboration should be lent to the camp project until certain improvements are made, both in the camp itself and in the attitude of the camp officials towards the various committees and their methods. I quite see that this attitude is very justifiable and, in ideal conditions, would probably have many desired results.
>
> On the other hand, knowing the very intransigent attitude which the camp authorities can take up – and which was in fact their only attitude up to about six months ago, when our help began to be appreciated and we were allowed to have more freedom in our contact with the refugees – I am perhaps rather afraid that if we, in our turn, become too intransigent, we may even find the camp is closed to us as they were to every Committee except the Quakers for a period of many months.
>
> This of course is perhaps too timid an attitude but I feel that the refugees will be in the end, as usual, the greatest sufferers of the affair. I am in complete agreement with you that the French

* The Nimes Coordinating Committee, so named because it held its meetings in that city, was set up to coordinate the work of the 25 national and international organisations working to help refugees in the camps. It met regularly from November 1940 until March 1943.

> Government is definitely concerned about the conditions of the camps and anxious to improve them. … But the problem of camp re-organisation is so tremendous and the possibility at present so very meagre that we cannot hope for any very startling improvement in the space of a very short time.

On 4 April Mary again wrote to Kershner, after he had been approached by Nimes Committee members:

> I am of course in agreement that we should not be bound by any conditions as regards the method of work which we would follow. I feel that there is a shade of coercion in the back of the minds of your visitors when they state that by making a combination our chance of working in the camps might be improved. I have a strong feeling that the matter could work in quite an opposite fashion.
>
> I feel that these other Committees are beginning at the wrong end in wishing to force an entry into the camps. The Quakers have never used this system and have never been refused either entry or circulation. I think it is extremely unlikely that the doors will be closed to us now and at Rivesaltes I feel that our distribution will take the natural evolution that they have taken at Argelès, i.e. both the setting up of different services and the distribution of our gifts will automatically take place through these services. … So far the things that I have sent to Rivesaltes have been such that they have naturally been given to the camp authorities. They were sheets for the crèche, babies' bottles, rubber sheeting, etc. … which no Committee would wish to personally hand out to each child. The milk which I have sent is being used at the discretion of the doctor and I am sure that you will agree that Dr Lefevre is a person who will use it at the best advantage.

Returning to her previous preoccupation with educational and cultural activities for the refugees, she outlined plans to set up a school and workrooms in Rivesaltes: "… the materials will, as at Argelès, be used for these services and, in the case of the clothing, distributed through work rooms. This is done at Argelès to the entire satisfaction of the French authorities and of the refugees."

In her AFSC report on the new camp, on 31 March, Mary noted that there were 233 fewer children in the camp compared with the February figure, explaining that this was due: "to the reunion of families with the father who is working outside the camp, either with a private employer or in the work company, to the return to Spain of other families and to the effort made by different organisations to place the children in colony groups outside the camp."

Her report shows almost thirty different nationalities were represented in the camp, with Spaniards still the most numerous among Greeks, Armenians, Turks, Swedes and others.

> Food conditions in the camp continue to be bad, but a certain improvement has been achieved since the inauguration of refectories for the adults. The distribution of the food, at least between the kitchens and the tin can of the internee, can at least be more strictly controlled and the quantity of food which ultimately reaches the latter is therefore a little more than previously. At first, the internees did not care for the idea of having to go to the refectory, but now they admit that it is more agreeable to eat seated at a table than huddled in their barracks as heretofore.
>
> The main substantial food of the children and of many of the grown-ups is still however the supplement distributed of [sic] Quaker rice and chickpea flour and other supplements supplied by the Swiss and other organisations.

She went on to explain that these supplements were prepared in the Secours Suisse barrack under the direction of one of its delegates and her assistants:

> The distribution takes place either in the barrack, where a section is railed off and furnished with benches so as to serve as sort of dining room, or in the infirmaries. The categories which come

to eat at the Secours Suisse/Quakers barrack are the children of school age, the adolescents, the auxiliary nurses and the workers of the 'ateliers' [workshops]. The ration is taken from the barrack to the infirmaries and to the special barracks for the children under the age of three years. The distributions take place from 8.30 in the morning to 4.30 in the afternoon.

The auxiliary nurses have recently been included in the distributions as the Medecin-Chef [Chief Medical Officer] found it impossible to recruit amongst the internees a sufficient number of women and girls to act as aides to the French Red Cross nurses in charge of the infirmaries and the Pouponnieres [day nurseries]. These girls have not been paid by the camp since the month of July last, although they work long hours in extremely difficult conditions and with few facilities; they only receive a very small piece of bread as an extra ration per day and finally refused to continue to work on plea that they were not able to make the effort on the small ration of food supplied by the camp.

In response, Mary explained, the Quakers, L'Oeuvre de Secours aux Enfants (OSE – a Jewish aid agency) and the Unitarian Service Committee had agreed to provide these workers with a small supplement of food from their own stocks and provide extra pocket money. Referring to the quantity of food supplied by the camp, she noted that: "It has been stated by the Delegate of the Secours Suisse that the ration actually allocated to each internee is sufficient, but owing to the many hands through which this quantity passes before reaching the internee it becomes a very inadequate daily ration."

Mary added that a special distribution of food had recently been started for the many internees suffering from cachexia, a disease that causes the body of those suffering from malnutrition to waste away.

The external manifestations are an extreme emaciation. In many cases, there are men over 5 feet 10 weighing between 40 and 45 kg … in some cases, weakness is so great that in the case of a fall the patient is incapable of getting up unaided. The patients

> are unable to maintain a standing position for longer than a few minutes and are incapable of all other forms of effort. Death occurs frequently for no special cause. Cold or heat often occasions the death of one of these persons who otherwise have not shown any other symptoms of a more serious nature than those indicated above.

Mary went on to explain that eleven special barracks had been allotted to accommodate the cachexia cases, most of whom were men. Three of these barracks were being used to treat the most serious cases and the camp authorities had agreed that Secours Suisse would be in charge of feeding these patients.

> The camp ration is handed over for preparation and is usually served at the midday meal. Breakfast, a mid-morning and afternoon snack is supplied by the different organisations working in the camp. As well as the distribution of rice and chickpea flour, the Quakers send 120 litres of milk to the camp daily for the patients of these three barracks and the others already mentioned housing the less serious cases. … In the three special barracks, as well as the feeding program, many of these patients are receiving a medical treatment in the form of special vitamin preparation supplied by the Unitarian Service Committee and obtained in Switzerland. It is interesting to note that during the six weeks … that the new program has operated all of the patients of the special barracks have gained weight, many of them as much as 1 or 2 kilos a week.

Mary then turned to the health of the children in the camp, noting that while there were currently no outbreaks of epidemics their general state of health was poor:

> Many of them are below weight, suffer from skin eruptions, boils etc. … due to poor food and almost total lack of hygiene. Many of them are dirty and unkempt although it is true that large numbers

> of the mothers make great efforts, in spite of the lack of water and soap, to keep their children clean and tidy.
>
> The condition of the clothing of the men, women and children is very bad. Many of the children have no underclothing and the same applies to men and women or if they do have certain of these articles, they have one of each and cannot wash these as frequently as they would like.

Mary's report highlighted the lack of proper footwear as a serious problem:

> Many of the internees are practically barefoot. The sandal workshop continues to work satisfactorily, but the output is relatively small owing to the difficulties of working up the poor quality of the material now available. Some 500 pairs were made during March, but unfortunately these were not enough to palliate the need for shoes. The life of the sandals, also owing to their poor quality, is relatively short.

In summer, the hard, flinty soil lacerated the internees' bare feet while winter rain turned the ground around the barracks into a freezing quagmire, through which people struggled to make headway. In due course Mary would arrange for an espadrille maker in the camp to make this basic footwear and to train others to do the same.

She had also overseen the setting up of a sewing workshop, although work on new garments had come to a halt "as the stock of material … are completely exhausted and irreplaceable. The women are employed in the remaking of old garments and the reutilization of wool which can be recuperated from sweaters etc. … already used by the internees."

She went on to say that other services provided by the aid workers included following up requests for release and efforts to hasten these demands but that the process of liaising with the prefects, through which all such requests had to pass, was a lengthy one.

Many of those who sought release from the camp hoped to emigrate to the United States – at that point one of the few countries still willing to take in immigrants. To the already complex procedures required to access the necessary visas for such a trip, the Vichy Government added an extra obstacle. As historian Alexendre Doulut notes, "Vichy put a ceiling of Fr25,000 on the amount of money an emigrant could take out of the camp. This sum would be almost swallowed up by the price of a voyage to the continent of America." This meant that the traveller would arrive at his destination with funds precariously low at a time when the host country was refusing entry to those without private means. A second limitation, stipulated in the Armistice, meant that male refugees of military age were barred from emigrating from France to those countries, such as Poland and Czechoslovakia, that were fighting Germany.

In the early stages of the camp's existence, some of the internees fortunate enough to have the financial wherewithal could obtain permission from the camp authorities to visit the village of Rivesaltes to supplement their camp rations by buying food directly from villagers or shopkeepers. It was not long, however, before the outraged local mayor issued a council edict banning this practice and urged Captain Humbert to put an immediate end to what he called "daily invasions of the village by shabby undesirables".

Many starving internees ignored this mayoral injunction and continued to visit the village without authorisation, despite the risk of being imprisoned in Perpignan if caught.

In April 1941, all 1,800 Jews in the camp were abruptly relocated to Block B, together with gypsy families, who were placed in different barracks. The camp authorities claimed this was to allow Jewish families to celebrate Passover together. The real reason had a far more sinister intent that would become clear the following summer. Block B was in much poorer condition than most of the other blocks, was over-run with rats and fleas, and lacked beds, so internees slept on straw mattresses on the floor. This block also received less food than the rest of the camp. As journalist and author Joel Mettay stated:

> According to various reports from that time this block was deliberately selected because it was situated about one kilometre from Block J ... where the milk ration [for children under ten] was

distributed. This meant that on very windy days or when it rained heavily the children, who were very weak, would not bother to go there.

The coming of summer, baking the arid plain at Rivesaltes, added another layer of suffering to the plight of the internees. Mosquitos joined the rats and other vermin swarming through the camp. Visitors were struck by the fetid stench from the latrines that pervaded the barracks day and night. In late June a report by the camp's medical inspectors noted the recurrent outbreak of epidemics due to malnutrition and bad hygiene practices among the internees, most of whom possessed only the clothes they had arrived in. "Of two hundred and forty infants in the camp sixty have died over the summer. In winter only the offices and the nurseries have heating."

By September Captain Humbert's report put the total number of internees at 4,979. The number of guards in the camp stood at 333. Figures for the food supply point to an excess of seasonal vegetables and an insufficiency of everything else. The daily ration of meat was set at less than 5g of meat per internee. Less than half a litre of milk was provided for each child. In censored letters the internees pleaded for help, telling those outside the camp how they had no clothes or shoes and were constantly hungry.

Through the prefect the Vichy authorities contributed Fr11.5 per day for each internee – a sum that in theory would enable those in the camp to obtain the same depleted food supply as people living outside the camp. In reality, the amount spent on daily food for the internees was only Fr7 or Fr8. As Joel Mettay points out in his book on the camp: "Those running the camp didn't try to disguise this fact. On the contrary they congratulated themselves for being such prudent managers! On the other hand it is not clear how these 'economies' were achieved."

George Koltein, who as a young boy was taken to the camp with his family, had this to say about the food in Rivesaltes:

> I have two memories which have marked my life .... We got a tiny piece of bread in the morning that you had to divide up for

> the day. Luckily, I didn't stay in the camp at Rivesaltes for long [George and his brother were taken out by Mary]. I've never eaten bread since that time. The second [memory] is that because it was August tomatoes were plentiful so we ate tomato soup. The skins were indigestible and would float in the toilet bucket. I've never eaten tomatoes since then.

Until the invasion of France the AFSC delegates there had been receiving regular shipments of food and used clothing from the United States to distribute to those in their care, both inside and outside the camps. But as Howard Wriggins recounts in his book *Picking Up the Pieces from Portugal to Palestine*, after France signed the 1940 Armistice with Germany, a British blockade prevented all direct shipments to France:

> If we obtained the proper documents from the British, order by order, it was still possible to ship to us in Portugal and for us to forward from there to our delegations in France [via the port of Marseille]. … The bulk shipments we managed to send were mainly for the refugees interned in the camps and for school feeding programs organized by our four *délégations*.

Malnourished, denied basic washing facilities and psychologically traumatised by their experiences, the men, women and children had lost all resistance to disease. Babies were particularly vulnerable: in July alone 23 infants died in the camp.

The difference of opinion between the majority of the committee members and Mary continued throughout the year, as a steady flow of new arrivals streamed into the camp. Despite the best efforts of Mary and her colleagues, conditions continued to deteriorate.

In November 1940 the International Red Cross was authorised to visit the camps in the south of France. Its report painted a sorry picture of life for the internees at Rivesaltes, citing an insufficient food supply, lack of hygiene, an infestation of rats, epidemics, ill-treatment and inadequate food. The AFSC's December monthly report stated:

> The internees are now going through a time of great suffering. Winter has finally descended on the region with the bitter winds that characterise it in this part of the Midi. To their miseries of hunger and lack of liberty is now that of cold. They are cold during the night, they are cold during the day and their food is served to them cold. They crouch in unheated barracks and have no extra blankets or clothes to protect them against the searching wind. There has been an almost entire lack of wood in the camp – the supply has been insufficient to cook the miserable soup that is served disguised as a meal. The infirmaries and nurseries are unheated and the ill and the babies shiver in their beds and their hands are covered with chilblains.

In November, Friedel Bohny-Reiter, a Vienna-born nurse working for the Secours Suisse, moved into the camp on a permanent basis. The diary she kept for the next twelve months provides a vivid insight into the hardships of daily life in the camp, both for the internees and those struggling to assist them. By December the food situation had deteriorated to such a degree that Captain Humbert calculated that one-third of internees were suffering from malnutrition. On Christmas Eve Friedel recorded that one Spanish woman told her that "there are nights when I cannot sleep because of the thought of food."

***

On 20 January 1942, senior Nazi party and government officials met in a villa in the Berlin suburb of Wannsee. The purpose of the meeting, convened by SS General Reinhard Heydrich, was to coordinate ways of implementing the so-called 'Final Solution to the Jewish Question' – an operation that envisioned nothing less than the total annihilation by the Nazis of some eleven million European Jews, including those not living in German-controlled territory. Just over two months later the first convoy of foreign Jews – targeting Jews arrested during round-ups in 1941 and held in the transit camps of Pithiviers and Beaune-la-Rolande or in Drancy – departed France for Auschwitz.

By the summer of 1942 Rivesaltes would become the major holding centre for Jews arrested in Vichy France and Mary and her colleagues would find themselves in a frantic race to save as many lives as possible.

The roles Mary was called upon to play in the camp were many and various, such as locating missing people among the internees or helping re-unite families – much as she had done in Argelès and the other camps before the opening of Rivesaltes. A typical example of this kind of work can be seen in a letter Mary received from the Marseille office at the end of April asking her to investigate the case of Joseph Katz, then interned at Rivesaltes:

> Monsieur Katz, whose wife died in the camp of Gurs, has four children in the United States who are doing everything possible to effect their father's emigration.
>
> Do you think it would be possible for M. Katz to be released? We would be very grateful if you could go to the camp of Rivesaltes and discuss the matter with him.

Over the course of the coming months Mary received hundreds of similar letters asking her to intercede on behalf of people in the camp. Despite the mounting pressure on her as the deportations loomed, Mary did her best to examine each case personally. In many of these cases her efforts bore fruit. Others, such as that of Joseph Katz, ended in tragedy: he was deported to his death from Rivesaltes on 9 September 1942.

A report to AFSC headquarters in Philadelphia, on 14 April 1942, by a Quaker visitor to Rivesaltes paints a stark picture of life in the camp for both the internees and Mary:

> From Perpignan it takes only about 15 or 20 minutes by car to reach the camp, but it is as though one had travelled in that short time to another world … rows of barracks stretching almost as far as the eye can see. The principal impression I got of the camp was one of bleakness and bareness. The barracks themselves are well constructed of concrete, with windows in them which is already something. They are set quite far apart, but nothing

grows on the earth surrounding them – there is only hard, bare, stony ground. There is no grass, no trees, nothing green to relieve the eyes from the monotony of the grey barracks and the sand coloured ground. … It is incredible that there could be so many stones on the ground as there are. … The sun was shining brightly and there was a strong wind blowing that made walking almost difficult, and the air was filled with flying dust and sand. It was rather like being in a desert – the glare was so terrific, and we walked around with our eyes squinted into slits. There were very few people to be seen as we made our way around the bleak and inhospitable place, and when I commented on this to Mary Elmes she explained that on the windy days almost everyone stays in the barracks all day as they haven't the strength to walk around against the force of the wind. The people we did see moved slowly and painfully as though they were bending all their efforts on the mere act of locomotion. There is apparently a great deal of wind at Rivesaltes that accounts in part for all the rocks and stones. It is very stony ground, and the wind is continually blowing all the loose top soil away. The climate is unfortunately very hard on young children; almost all of the mothers with whom I have talked and who have been in several camps said that Rivesaltes was the worst of all for the children, because of the climate and the constant wind. The children's faces are all rough and chapped, and their cheeks looked spuriously rosey, with the rosiness that does not come from health, unfortunately; they squint against the unrelieved glare of the sun, from which they have no protection of shade trees, awnings or dark glasses. We watched the children having their 4 o'clock meal of our rice and the Secours Suisse milk and a little 'paté-de-fruit' furnished by the OSE. The barrack is arranged with the kitchen at one end, space for storing the food at the other end, and in the middle a space with benches where the children sit to eat the meal. … The children lined up outside the barrack in long lines, each child with a tin can or a pail or some other homely receptacle for the food in his hand, and a spoon in his pocket. The barrack is white-washed on the outside and

> has pictures painted on it. Around the doorway by which the children enter is painted a picture of a Secours Suisse train, and OSE truck … and a Quaker ship – each coming laden with food for the barrack. The Quaker ship has a large American flag on its outside. … As I looked at it, and then looked at the children standing patiently in line, buffeted by the wind, waiting to receive their daily ration, the tears came to my eyes to think the ships are not coming from America with good food for the sad little children. I think that if the powers that arrange these things could have stood by my side and seen the thin malformed little bodies and the wistful screwed-up little faces of these children they might wish to reconsider their policy. …
>
> The thing that struck me most forcibly as I looked at them individually was not the fact that they were so wretchedly clad; not that their feet were protected from the stony ground by shoes clumsily made out of blankets or straw; not even the stooped shoulders, the thin legs, the sores that do not heal and the blueness around the eyes. I was prepared for the sight of all these things, but what I was not prepared for was the expression on the faces of all these children. The intentness, the deadly seriousness with which they approach their turn to be served from the steaming kettle filled with a thick mixture of rice and milk. With absolute concentration they watched while the big ladle full of rice was put into the container which they held forward to receive it. And if a few grains of the precious rice got on the outside of the pail they immediately licked it up, so that they would not lose one grain. …
>
> There was no talking, no laughing, not even smiling faces – no noise from the children except the scraping of the spoon in the pails. … And it was the brooding … faces of the little children scraping up the last bit of the small ration which we can give them that really moved me most of all ….

The visitor went on explain that he had learned from one of the teachers that when the kindergarten first opened the children drew only barracks, not knowing any other subject to draw, before continuing:

> Now, through the introduction of picture books and stories, they are getting an idea of houses and trees, of animals and trains. Another teacher related that she had made a border around one of the walls of her room with drawings of rabbits. When the children first came in and saw them they were frightened, thinking that they were rats, as that was the only animal of that kind with which they had had any acquaintance. Really, the intellectual poverty and the psychological deprivation of the camp environment are such that it can hardly bear thinking on. What kind of adults can we expect these half-starved, captive children to grow up to be?
>
> I saw other facets of our work at Rivesaltes, too – the atelier for making extra espadrilles which Mary Elmes has recently started, the feeding for the adolescent group of children, and the feeding of the group of so-called 'cachetiques', people who have suffered from undernourishment to such an extent that they are almost ready to die. The barracks for these men, old and young, is a sight which one cannot easily forget … on the second day the wind had died down, and the people came out of the barracks to be in the sun. Unfortunately there is no place at all to sit outside except for the small doorstep on the front of each barrack – otherwise one must sit down on the ground. Everywhere Mary Elmes went she was greeted with great warmth and affection and could not walk very far without being stopped by someone who wished to talk to her. One could see very plainly that 'Miss Mary', as they call her, brought joy to many people on her regular frequent visits to the camp.

Earlier in the year Friedel Bohny-Reiter had been shocked to discover that food was so scarce that doctors in the camp were trying to nourish starving people by giving them vitamin injections instead of food of any kind. Inevitably scores of people died from this 'treatment', which eerily prefigures the experiments the Nazi Dr Josef Mengele performed on Jewish prisoners in Auschwitz.

In June the drinking water supply to the camp became contaminated by the latrines, prompting fears of yet another outbreak of epidemic disease. Separately, the Chief Medical Officer had urged aid agencies to take children younger than one year old out of the camp ahead of the worst of the summer heat and place them in colonies. Since the first deportations from Paris had already begun it was known to be just a matter of time before the Jews in Rivesaltes suffered a similar fate so the medical officer's suggestion was seized upon by Mary and her colleagues as the perfect pretext to extricate infant Jewish children from the camp.

On 16 July 1942 Friedel noted the arrival of 'black cars' at the camp, unaware that the German officials included SS officer Theodor Dannecker, who was making a tour of the camps in the Unoccupied Zone to make an inventory of the Jews being held. July also saw the arrival in the camp of Jews arrested in the Unoccupied Zone, adding to the sense of fear among the internees. On 3 August events unexpectedly took a dramatic turn for the worse. In a postscript to a letter she had just written that day to Eleanor Cohu, of the AFSC's Marseille office, Mary broke the news:

> We are in a state of turmoil here at Rivesaltes. All the Jews have been today placed in a special îlot [jail block] and there are rumours that they are to be sent to an unknown destination. Orders from above. A new census has been made and anything may happen. I presume the same events are taking place in other camps.

From then on the Jews would live in Blocks F and K, surrounded by a double fence of barbed wire and extra guards, in conditions even worse than those in Block B, conveniently grouped together when the time came for them to be taken away.

5

Raids at Dawn

In the early hours of 16 July 1942, 4,500 French police fanned out through the streets of Paris to launch a massive round-up of Jews. In homes all over the city thousands of Jewish families were startled from their sleep by a hammering on their doors. Bleary-eyed and apprehensive, they were given minutes to dress before being escorted into the street and taken away. Most never saw their homes again. The round-up, codenamed *Opération Vent Printanier* (Spring Wind), continued into the following day. As evening settled over Paris on the first day of the round-ups more than 11,000 Jews had been detained. By the end of the second day the number of those arrested rose to 13,000 – much to the disappointment of the German authorities who had been supplied by French police chiefs with the names and addresses of 25,000 Jews. Many of those who evaded capture had been tipped off about the impending raids by sympathetic gendarmes or neighbours. Rumours of a round-up had led thousands of Jewish men to go into hiding before the raid, believing that women and children were not the intended targets. As a result, the highest proportion of those arrested were women and children. Over the two-day operation a total of more than 4,000 children were arrested and deported to their deaths. The round-ups had been planned with the aid of the head of the French police, Réné Bousquet, and the self-styled Louis Darquier de Pellepoix, a self-serving, rabid anti-Semite who had been receiving money from the Nazi party in Berlin throughout the 1930s in return for inciting anti-Jewish sentiment in France. By the time of the round-ups Darquier had been appointed Commissioner for Jewish Affairs by the Vichy Government. German officers overseeing the raids included SS Captain Dannecker, head of the Nazis' Jewish section in France. Operation Spring Wind had originally been planned to take place between 13 and 15 July but was re-scheduled to avoid coinciding with Bastille Day, France's national holiday.

Of those captured in the raids, 6,000 were loaded onto public buses and driven to the holding camp at Drancy, in the suburbs north of the city. The unfinished multi-storey buildings at Drancy had originally been planned as social housing units, a project considered enlightened by contemporary observers. Now its role became that of a holding centre for Jews marked for deportation. Today at Drancy stands a memorial to the Jews who were held there until they were sent to the east by the trainload. In a small cobbled area a plaque marks the spot where three separate teams, working day and night for months, burrowed through the soil in a desperate bid for freedom. They were just three metres away from freedom when the escape plot was discovered. All those involved were shot.

In the Unoccupied Zone, the camp of Rivesaltes performed a similar role to its Paris counterpart by interning Jews caught in Vichy France until they could be deported, leading eminent Holocaust historian Serge Klarsfeld to label it "the Drancy of the south."

About 7,000 of those arrested in the July round-up (parents with children under sixteen) were taken to the Velodrome d'Hiver, an indoor cycling stadium, known as the Vel d'Hiv, on the Boulevard de Grenelle in Paris's 15th arrondisement. The remainer of those arrested in the raid were taken to internment camps, with the majority being held in Drancy. For five days the detainees were held in conditions of squalor. The authorities' policy of splitting up families meant that 4,000 children were separated from their parents and eventually deported, among strangers, to their deaths in Auschwitz. In the Vel d'Hiv stadium the terrified detainees sweltered in the July heat under its sealed glass roof. The only facilities in the stadium were one tap and three toilets, forcing people to forego their dignity and relieve themselves in public. Some of those incarcerated committed suicide by throwing themselves from the top tiers of the stadium; others escaped by bribing guards. As a special correspondent for the British newspaper *The Guardian* reported:

The hunt for Jews was relentless, not a single soul whom the police could lay hands on was allowed to go free. Inmates of the Rothschild Hospital, which had been set apart for patients [already interned at Drancy] ... were placed under arrest regardless of their condition and no matter how recently they had been operated upon. Children over three years old were separated from their mothers, about 5,000 of them being herded together into school buildings, wither they were taken in lorries after their parents had been seized from their homes and locked up by police. Quite a number of smaller children were unable to give their names and cannot be identified.

Efforts are now being made by the Quakers, the Salvation Army and the Israelite Union of France to improve conditions in the camps. ... The prisoners are half starved and deprived of the most elementary comforts. There is no proper sanitation, no medical supplies and no kitchen equipment. ...

The plight of the French Jews was relieved to some extent by the help and sympathy shown to them by their non-Jewish countrymen. Some were enabled to escape and numbers of children were given shelter and smuggled later into the unoccupied territory [Vichy France] in spite of the danger involved. Others who evaded arrest are trying desperately to reach unoccupied France and there is an almost uninterrupted stream of fugitives towards the demarcation line.

One such fugitive was George Koltein, a seven-year-old who lived with his parents and brother in a cramped apartment in the 20th arrondissement of Paris – an area of the city popular among the waves of immigrants who began arriving in the French capital in the middle of the nineteenth century. His parents, both Polish Jews, had married in Paris in the 1920s and worked from home as tailors. "I don't know how, but my parents knew there was going to be a raid", George remembered. "When the French police came knocking at our apartment door my mother didn't open it. We were very lucky that they didn't break down the door." Guessing, correctly, that the police would return, the family went downstairs to a neighbour, an Italian who had moved to Paris in preference to living under Mussolini's fascist regime. He invited the Kolteins into his apartment and hid them in his kitchen. The police returned to raid the building a second time some hours later. This time they did break down the Kolteins' door. Finding the apartment deserted the police began banging on other doors and eventually came to their Italian neighbour's apartment. The terrified family huddled in their neighbour's tiny kitchen and listened as he calmly assured the policemen that the Kolteins had left early that morning. Satisfied that the Koltein family had indeed fled, the police went in search of other victims.

George's mother had a sister living on the other side of the city with her husband. Their Italian neighbour offered to cross Paris to find out how they had fared and returned with the news that George's aunt and uncle had been taken in the raid and were in Drancy, pending their deportation to Auschwitz. They were both murdered shortly after arriving in Poland.

Since it was unlikely that his aunt's apartment would be raided again, the Kolteins made the nerve-wracking journey across Paris and hid there for a few days while they planned their next move. With the help of the concierge they found a passeur, or guide, who, for a hefty fee, was willing to take them over the demarcation line into the Unoccupied Zone.

"When we crossed the demarcation line we were arrested on the other side by French police. It was then that my mother, my brother and myself were taken to Rivesaltes and my father put into a Foreign Workers Company." After a few weeks George's father was seconded from his work company and sent to assist a tailor in a small village near Limoges. In late August Mary approached George's mother, who agreed to give her custody of her son and his older brother, Jacques, so that the boys could be taken from the camp and transferred to the Villa St Christophe, a convalescent home for children at Canet-le-Plage, twenty kilometres from Rivesaltes.

The Villa St Christophe had been set up by Lois Gunden, a 27-year-old American member of the Mennonite Central Committee. In the wake of the Retirada Mary had used the villa to house Spanish children from the camps and enjoyed a good relationship with Lois, who came to regard the Irishwoman as a mentor.

Of his time at Canet-la-Plage George recalled: "I have only happy memories of Canet, playing on the beach in the sun." When his mother secured her release from Rivesaltes in September 1942 she rented a small apartment near the colony so that she would be near her two sons. Later she moved to Limoges to be with her husband. "In July 1943 we left the colony and went to live with them. We lived there until we returned to Paris in 1945."

In the village nobody bothered the new arrivals, even though George's parents spoke French with heavy Eastern European accents and were obviously Jewish. "I found out later that the local mayor was a *résistant*. The whole area had a strong Resistance presence."

At the end of 1943 all those who had been seconded to outside jobs were ordered to return to their work companies. George's father went into hiding, moving from farm to farm, paying his way by renovating his hosts' worn-out clothes. Three months before the Liberation of Paris he returned to live with his family and although the local police knew of his presence in the village the family was left in peace.

> When I got out of Rivesaltes camp, it was Mary Elmes who took us to the Maison St Christophe because in Lois Gunden's diary we find this entry that Mary Elmes has driven seven Jewish children to this house and I'm certain that I was one of those seven children. What we can say is that Mary Elmes, like Lois Gunden, formed part of a chain of solidarity that came to the aid of Jews. And luckily they did.

The July round-ups prompted an unprecedented flood of Jews into the Unoccupied Zone, putting yet more pressure on the relief agencies. The OSE reported taking into its care 800 children who had managed to make their way over the demarcation line. SS Captain Dannecker's July tour of the camps in the Unoccupied Zone formed part of measures to take a census of internees and members of foreign workers companies. Every internee had to supply detailed information on the composition of their families and the whereabouts of any relatives living outside the camps.

A report by Ross McClelland, a member of the AFSC's Marseille delegation, provides an illuminating insight not only into the activities of the relief agencies but also casts light on the mind-set of key members in the Vichy regime.† He notes that on 1 August 1942 a special meeting of the Nimes Committee was held at the Marseille offices of the YMCA. There he learned that 3,600 Jewish internees at the camps of Gurs (near Pau) and Rivesaltes were to be sent to the Occupied Zone on trains scheduled to leave between 6 and 12 August.

> The order applied to all foreign Jews – men, women and children – who had entered France after January 1, 1936. A few days later we heard from the Quaker office in Toulouse that convoys were also to be sent from the camps of Récebédou and Noé. …
>
> The Coordinating Committee took a unanimous decision that representatives should go personally to Vichy and attempt to see Marshal Pétain to protest this action formally and emphatically, and, if it could not be stopped, to seek the exemption of at least certain categories of internees, notably children under the age of 16, all those in possession of immigration visas or visa authorisations for the United States, and persons working for the relief organizations assisting France in coping with the problem of foreign refugees. If the Vichy authorities remained adamant, the relief committees should request that qualified representatives of such accepted relief organizations as the International Committee of the Red Cross be permitted access to the deportees wherever they might be sent.

The following day Lindsley Noble, Howard Kershner's successor at the AFSC, called a meeting of all its members, at which it was decided that he and Ross McClelland should travel to Vichy as soon as possible to

† The extracts from Ross McClelland's report quoted here are from the United States Holocaust Memorial Museum Collection, gifted to them by his son, Kirk McClelland, and have only recently been released.

request a meeting with Pétain and Prime Minister Pierre Laval. The fact that the first transports were scheduled to depart from the Unoccupied Zone on 6 August lent added urgency to their mission.

> It was agreed that our plea to stop this unacceptable action should be made primarily on humanitarian and religious grounds and secondarily, if necessary, on the political grounds that such acquiescence on the part of the French government in the Nazis' designs to the treatment of Jewish refugees in France could have serious repercussions in the United States which could jeopardize the larger Quaker relief program in France for needy French and foreign alike.

On 4 August Ross and Lindsley arrived in Vichy for a meeting with Dr Bernard Ménétral, Pétain's physician and private secretary, but were unable to see him until the following day.

> At the hotel we ran into Tracy Strong, Sr, of the World's YMCA .... He told us he was scheduled to see Pétain later in the afternoon to discuss prisoner-of-war package matters. We briefed him rapidly on the impending deportation of foreign Jews from France and asked him to impress, if possible, on the Marshal, the highly adverse impact this development could have on the future of American relief operations in occupied France. Mr Strong later reported to us that his discussion on this subject with Pétain had been very unsatisfactory since the old man seemed largely unaware of what was happening. He was primarily concerned with the worsening food situation in France, and the mention of the deportation measures elicited only the repeated observation from him: 'Les Allemands sont durs!' (The Germans are hard).

The two AFSC men met Dr Ménétral the following day and explained the reason for their visit:

> ... we could see that he was deeply distressed. In responding, however, he somewhat arbitrarily separated the humanitarian

basis of our appeal for a mitigation of the harsh deportation order from what he presented as France's increasingly difficult internal situation under the German occupation. ... Ménétral advanced arguments which we were to hear from several levels of the Vichy government in our ensuing talks. The foreign Jews were France's misfortune, a misfortune for which the Blum Popular Front Government was primarily to blame for having let down the bars to the entry of thousands of them, Ménétral contended. They rapidly became focal points of anti-government propaganda, of Communist agitation, and of black market activity in derogation of the asylum France had granted them. France had never wanted them, could not assimilate them. He taxed the United States with having done miserably little to help France with the situation or to take these refugees in. In response to our demur that a number of American organisations such as our own had on the contrary done a great deal to help France in coping with this admitted problem, especially in the internment camps in favour of refugee children, Ménétral conceded that this was indeed true, but went on to inform us that the Germans now seemed willing to take these people back, having decided to place them all in a 'Jewish reservation' in southern Poland, where families would be reunited and they could all live and work together. We protested that the brutal steps that had been taken in Paris, of which he must be aware, to break up foreign Jewish families and separate them into various categories – the able-bodied, the old and ill, the young girls, and the children – hardly supported the Nazi contention that they were 'regrouping families' but seemed to us designed to serve some far more sinister purpose. Based on the information increasingly filtering out of Eastern Europe we said we feared that the true purpose was physical annihilation. Dr Ménétral brushed off this interpretation as a hysterical exaggeration. At the close of our difficult talk Ménétral indicated, although he did not say so in so many words, that there was little point in our trying to talk to Marshal Petain about this painful subject. The person to see was Prime Minister Laval. He said he would probably have a chance

> to talk to the latter at lunch and would attempt to get the Prime Minister to receive us.

That afternoon Ross was advised by the doctor to contact a M. Villars, a member of Laval's 'personal cabinet', whom they met the following day:

> He appeared to know little about either the tragic lot of foreign refugees in France (he characterised the Spanish refugees from the Civil War along with the Jews as inveterate troublemakers), the relief work of the various foreign organizations trying to help France with these refugee problems, or about deportation back into German hands of the foreign Jews.

M. Villars' office in the Hotel du Parc was one floor below that of Dr Ménétral, whom the pair had arranged to meet again around noon. Upstairs, on their way to meet the doctor, Ross and Lindsley bumped into the prime minister:

> We saw Laval, Ménétral and one or two other men standing at the end [of the corridor]. Seeing us approaching Ménétral immediately said a word to Laval, and beckoned to us. The four of us – Laval (olive complexion, haggard and sallow, black head of hair and the inevitable white string cravatte [sic]), Ménétral, Lindsley and I – stepped into an adjoining office ....
>
> Laval was clearly impatient, and harassed. He launched forthwith into a tirade against the foreign Jews who France received. They constituted an undesirable element ... a source of anti-government agitation, and black-market activity. The French Government had not wanted them in the first place and asked nothing better now then to 'get rid of them' .... This decision fortunately coincided with the present German policy of taking them back in order to establish 'an ethnic reservation' and 'special centres' in Poland where the Jews would be gathered together to live and work.

At this point Dr Ménétral interjected to disagree with the prime minister, offering his view that the real motive behind the deportations was the extermination of the Jews.

> Laval, waved this aside as 'preposterous', 'pure fiction'. He continued in an interrogatory tone to ask us why it was, if our government was so 'pro-semitic', that the United States did not admit these refugees instead of criticising France for the way she treated them.

Laval then voiced similar criticisms of the British Government, before going on to denounce foreign Jews as internationalists in the sense that they never wished to become good citizens of any country. As such, they have done more harm to France than good, and had moreover shown themselves to be 'ingrates' (ungrateful) in the face of France's hospitality. In contrast to his denunciation of foreign Jews, the prime minister adopted a more measured approach to those who were French citizens:

> As far as French Jews were concerned, Laval went on significantly, that was another question. They were born in France and were consequently France's responsibility ....
>
> Although Laval was becoming increasingly impatient, we again emphasised the grave danger that Nazi policy towards Jews in general represented for their safety, indeed their survival, implying that French Jews as well were not necessarily safe in the long run. Laval snapped out: 'Maybe so. All the more reason therefore, to let them have the foreign Jews now in order to protect our own Jews.'

At this point Ross and Lindsley pleaded with Laval to have those foreign Jews in possession of US immigration visas, and who were due to leave within the next six weeks, to be exempted from the transports. "Laval would not go beyond saying that the matter was 'under consideration'." They then pressed the prime minister as to whether he would urgently consider exempting from the convoys children under the age of sixteen, but to no avail:

> At this juncture, Laval was urgently summoned, so we got no answer to our appeal for the children.
>
> As we stepped out into the corridor with Dr Ménétral, Marshal Pétain was just walking out of the old-fashioned grilled elevator … and Ménétral presented us to him. After a moment's hesitation, Pétain seemed to understand that we represented 'les Quakers Américans' (he had once met Lindsley's predecessor Howard Kershner.) Shaking our hands, he moved on down the corridor towards his office since Ménétral's look clearly indicated to us that we should not try to engage the old man in any substantive conversation.
>
> Lindsley and I returned to the Hotel des Ambassadeurs, where we were staying, in a very depressed frame of mind.

Meanwhile, in Rivesaltes, Mary was doing all she could for those threatened by the looming deportations. On 3 August she wrote to Una Mortished at the AFSC Marseille office:

> I have been asked by Alice Bodenheimer, Ilot J, bar. 37, Rivesaltes, if it would be possible to get in touch with her brother, Ernst Bodenheimer … [in Ohio]. She has heard nothing from him since last March and is very anxious to know at what stage are the negotiations for the obtaining of her emigration papers.

Alice Bodenheimer was deported to Auschwitz from Rivesaltes on 16 September 1942.

An impression of the connections Mary formed with those held in the camp emerges in a letter she wrote, again to her colleague in Marseille, on the day the first transport left from the Unoccupied Zone:

> In reply to your letter of August 4th, I know Clara Rothschild quite well and I have recently paid 2 transfers of money from America.

She is a very old woman and somewhat enfeebled, but appears well looked after by someone whom I think is her daughter and who accompanies her everywhere. I have not been able to discover so far if she has been comprised [included] in the group which has been separated from the rest of the camp or whether her age and bad health have exempted her but I am under the impression that any general rule against the Jews will affect all of them, whether young or old, well and ill.

6

Deportation

On 6 August 1942 Ross and Lindsley met with Tyler Thompson, the US Embassy's Political Counselor, who, unsurprisingly, was most interested in the account of their talks, especially with Prime Minister Laval, and offered to transmit any message they had for the AFSC in Philadelphia through secure State Department channels.

> We accepted his offer with alacrity since we seriously doubted that any open telegram on the subject would clear the Vichy censors. Thompson added that he knew the State Department would also be interested in the information we had obtained about Laval's knuckling down to the Germans in the deportation matter.

Later that day the two men went again to see M. Villars of Laval's office, who had invited them to continue their earlier conversation once he had been able to "inform myself more fully on the question". When it soon became apparent that in the interim M. Villars had been instructed to say nothing further about the deportation of foreign Jews, Ross and Lindsley ended the meeting. That night, after sending their cable to the AFSC, Lindsley left for Geneva while Ross caught the evening train back to Marseille.

> Shortly after getting to the office … next morning, Helga Holbek telephoned to tell us that the first group of 1,000 internees (ranging in ages from 18 to 86!) from the camp of Gurs had been loaded between mid-night and 5 a.m. the night before into 33 box-cars

> at the station of Oloron-St-Marie in the Basse Pyrenées and dispatched toward an unknown destination. Helga was terribly shaken and wept as she told us how the hopeful cry of 'Die Quaeker sind hier' [the Quakers are here] had spread from lip-to-lip as she drove into the low-lying, dreary camp that had already seen so much suffering among Spanish Republican refugees. Yet, other than pressing departing hands, taking a hastily scrawled message for loved-ones elsewhere, and trying desperately to spread a word of cheer, Helga said there had been little she could do to respond to the anguished confidence placed in her and the Quakers.

On 11 August the first convoy of refugees left the camp of Rivesaltes. The 400 foreign Jews chosen for the journey were loaded onto trucks and ferried to the train station a short distance away. In the station the train that would take them on the two-day journey north to Drancy was hitched to one carrying Jews from the camps of Noé and Récébédou, which had been kept in a siding since the previous evening. En route north the train would take on prisoners from the internment camp at Les Milles in Aix-en-Provence, taking the number of those in the transport to 982. As the prisoners were being bundled aboard by policemen, shocked villagers watched in disbelief as a scene of heartbreak and pandemonium unfolded. Joel Mettay described how events unfolded in *L'Archipel du Mépris*:

> The first transport left from the train station in Rivesaltes. The people were taken on trucks to the station. When they got out of the trucks to board the trains there were terrible scenes. The Jews knew perfectly well what was going to happen to them. So, other people definitely knew what was going on, perhaps not the general public, but the population of Rivesaltes saw these people trying to escape, [people] who didn't want to go on the train. Some people were trying to commit suicide, there were children. Rumours spread among the townspeople and that's why, afterwards, a spur-line was built from the camp to the main line that goes to Narbonne and the north, so that deportees could be

> transported directly from inside the camp. In this way the towns-people wouldn't witness these scenes again.

Many French officials harboured the view that all Jews were fabulously wealthy and possessed valuable jewellery and money. Wasting no time in appropriating any such assets for the state, an official from the prefecture contacted Captain Humbert on the day of the first transport to remind him that anything of value left behind by those being deported was henceforth to be considered the property of the Interior Ministry.

The train arrived at Drancy at 8 a.m. on 12 August after its hapless passengers had endured a journey of a day and a night in unspeakable conditions. As Alexandre Doulut points out, two days later a transport of 749 people departed for Auschwitz in cattle trucks, which included 395 people from Rivesaltes.

> This period is the worst in the history of the camp [of Drancy] for at least two reasons. First, never did so many internees enter the camp in so short a short time, and, consequently, the deportees were never so numerous as during that summer: more than 21,000 left Drancy for Auschwitz-Birkenau between August 10 and September 30 1942.

This period also saw the deportation from Drancy of the first of the Jewish children. On arrival at Auschwitz a selection was made by the camp authorities among the 991 people in the convoy. Of these, 115 men were chosen for labour duties. The remainder, including women and children, were immediately sent to the gas chamber.

Jacob Goldschmidt, whom Mary had been assisting in his efforts to emigrate to the United States, was one of those on the train who had been taken from the camp at Rivesaltes. Of the 400 people in his group he alone would survive, as Mary explained in a letter of 13 August to Andrée Montagnon of the AFSC's Marseille office:

> This man, who was on the convoy to Poland, has been sent back from Lyon [under police escort] to the camp of Rivesaltes. He has

a convocation from the American Consulate and all his papers for emigration are in order.

Would you be kind enough to see with the HICEM [a Jewish relief agency specialising in emigration efforts] what has been done for such cases and let me know as soon as possible. I am going to the camp this afternoon, where I shall see the list of the other men in the same situation and I shall forward it to you tomorrow morning.

Mr Goldschmidt was transferred from the camp to St Louis Hospital on 26 September, before being officially released on 10 November 1942.

After months of fearful speculation, convoys to the death camps were now a reality. Mary quickly moved to save as many people from the camp as she could. In a follow-up letter to Marseille that very day she wrote:

I enclose a list of persons in Rivesaltes whose papers are fairly advanced as regards their emigration to the United States. Those who are noted as having received convocations, have already been convoked at the end of last month by the American Consulate in Marseille and have in their possession the papers required by the Consulate.

Application has been made at the camp for their 'visa de sortie' [exit visa] and their 'sauf conduit' [safe conduct] to Marseille. The HICEM has in its possession the dossiers of all these cases, but I would be much obliged if you could see what can be done for them in Marseille. It is extremely regrettable and tragic that three persons who had their papers in the same state as Mr Goldschmidt left in the recent convoy. I was myself unfortunately not aware that they were in it and apparently the HICEM was not able to do anything to have them withdrawn before it was too late.

In view of the fact that the people on the list may again be menaced with a similar deportation, I wonder if the Delegates in the Marseille office could ask the Quakers in Philadelphia to

> make the most urgent demarches at Washington so that they may be helped to leave as soon as possible.
>
> I am sure you will understand the critical situation these poor people are in at present.

Among the other internees anxiously awaiting news about their emigration status was Sylvia Cohn, a 38-year-old from Offenburg in Germany. Mary had been communicating with the Marseille office about Sylvia's case for some time and on 22 August wrote to her colleagues:

> I passed your letter on to Mme Cohn and she tells me that all her papers are at Vichy, awaiting her exit visa. She has however received a letter from the Portuguese Consul stating that within 48 hours of presenting of her documents to him he will give her a transit visa. The most important matter now is the obtaining of her exit visa from France. I hope that a favourable answer on this point for her as well as for the others has been received by the HICEM from Vichy and I hope that something will be done urgently for her as she has been again already placed in a group of people whose departure is imminent and this time nothing will be possible to exclude her, except the reception of her exit visa and other papers in order.
>
> I should be greatly obliged if anything can be done by you from Marseille to hasten a decision in her case.

Despite the frantic efforts of Mary, her colleagues and the sympathetic Portuguese officials who had offered her the chance of escape with a transit visa, Sylvia was included on the transport from Rivesaltes on 14 September. Just over two weeks later she was murdered in Auschwitz.

A graphic sense of the atmosphere surrounding the preparations for the departures of the convoys emerges from Ross McClelland's report. Here he describes the departure of the first transport from Les Milles on 10–11 August 1942:

The selection of the first convoy began late in the afternoon and made a Dantesque scene of heat, confusion and apprehension, with the whole camp population assembled in the courtyard. There was a constant coming and going as people whose names had been called out were moved from one group to another escorted by Milice [paramilitary police officers] with carbines slung over their shoulders. Those not yet summoned were cordoned off to one side while those already designated were formed up in 'squads' of 20 to 30 people. Piles of suitcases, bags and bundles of the internees' meagre possessions were everywhere on the ground. Despite the late summer afternoon heat, many had overcoats on, fearful no doubt that they might need them in the winters of their destination. The stretchers were plying back and forth to the camp infirmary with the limp figures of the weak and old who had fainted in the confusion. The guards were even escorting people back and forth in one last act of indignity, to the camp latrines. …

Each car was loaded slowly and painfully, with the family groups kept together in so far as possible. About a foot of fresh straw covered the floor of each wagon, but the only ventilation consisted of the barred, rectangular openings (perhaps two feet long and a foot high) at each end of the car up near the roof (people had to pull themselves up by the bars, however, to talk through them). We began our distribution of boxes of sardines, pieces of soap, cans of condensed milk and small packets of sugar about 7 o'clock [in the evening] ….

People would call out to us repeatedly from the vents of the loaded cars with last minute messages for children still in Marseille; or a hand would thrust out a note with an address on it … occasionally, some crumpled banknotes or a piece of jewelry would be thrust through the bars with the sole remark: 'Für die Quaeker.' The hot smell of hay and closely packed human bodies struck your face as you got as close to the vent as possible to hear what was being said; and one would catch a glimpse, for the last time, of a strained familiar face in the light of your flashlight.

After snatching a few hours' sleep Ross and his colleagues returned to see the train set off:

> At first light we are all back at the siding. Soup from a large camp cauldron is being ladled out through the partly opened freight-car doors. We hate to see some of the old familiar faces again, especially in the clear summer morning light. Here is Richard F, for example, a young and talented German violinist. He has been named 'chef the wagon' and is taking his duties very seriously: helping the old people, cajoling the fainthearted, trying to establish some order within his small and special domain, counting the number of parcels to see that everyone has got one. He has talked the guards into opening the door so that the night buckets can be emptied. He smiles out at us. … For him this going was in some way a release, a liberation from the drab and crowded boredom of over two years of camp life, of never being alone to practice, of being half sick and constantly hungry, of the eternal waiting and hoping that a visa would finally come. What was happening now was at least a positive change, whatever fate might await him; indeed, he seemed almost to welcome it.‡

After the train finally left the siding Ross and his colleagues pondered the real reason for the transports:

> We sat a long time afterwards trying to find some half-way logical reason for the taking of these people by the Nazi authorities. It had been explained to us in Vichy, we noted, as 'ethnic regrouping' in Poland, the creation of some sort of a reserve where all the Jews would work and live together, an extension, as it were, of the time-honored Eastern European ghetto system. This seemed conceivable. On the other hand there was a gnawing fear in the back of our minds that some far more sinister fate awaited them.

‡ Richard Freund was a cousin of Hans Freund, the father of Réné and Mario – two of the boys Mary took out of Rivesaltes. Richard died in Auschwitz.

> Although the conceptual gap between a policy of forced-labor and outright extermination was hard for the mind to bridge .... Yet, the labor element could hardly be predominant since out of the 400 Jewish internees who had been deported in the first convoy from the camp at Rivesaltes, for example, it was obvious that at most 25 people were in good enough physical condition to be capable of any significant manual work.

Beginning with the very first deportations, the German authorities had laid down strict quotas for the number of Jews to be included in each convoy. The figures for these quotas were sent directly from Paris to Vichy, who passed them on the local prefects. If people bound for Drancy managed to evade the convoy or if, for any other reason, the number fell short of the quota police on the ground arbitrarily chose others to make up the shortfall. Now at Les Milles, just as Mary was doing at Rivesaltes, Ross and Lindsley approached the camp commandant in an attempt to have people with American visas removed from the convoy:

> We had a talk with the Commandant, who was obviously shocked and distressed by the forbidding implications of the action while he tried to cope with the disheartening business of drawing up the first lists of those to be deported. We told him we were preparing, and would bring him shortly, a list of those internees holding American visas, and pled [sic] with him to keep these people off his list for the time being. He said he would do all he could, but that the quotas for deportees imposed on him by the prefect were very rigid.
>
> There were – it should be recounted – many instances of compassion and goodwill on the part of French officials forced by circumstances to participate in this deportation action. More than one commandant of a Foreign Workers Company, for example, when he learned that the 'Milice' were coming to seal off the camp, told as many of his workers as he dared simply to 'scram'. When the commandant at the camp of Rivesaltes ... learned that the children would probably be deported, although they were not

> to be included at the outset, he simply 'gave' the children to our delegate [Mary Elmes] with the urgent admonition: 'Faites-les disparaitre!' [Make them disappear].

On the subject of quotas, Ross recounts a poignant vignette as told to him by Helga Holbek, Mary's opposite number in Toulouse, whose remit covered the notorious camp of Gurs:

> Helga said she had come upon two old ladies in their eighties waiting patiently [for the train], with their bags packed beside them, to be included in the convoy. When they were told they were well over the age limit of those slated for the list, they replied calmly that they wished to be included as volunteers so that some younger person might be excluded. Since they refused to go back to their barrack, Helga got some blankets to wrap them in and left them waiting serenely side-by-side for the loading.

On 10 August a convoy of 120 internees from the camps at Noé and Récébédou rolled into the railway station at Rivesaltes, shortly before midnight. Those on board spent the night crammed aboard the train, with nothing to eat but the rations given to them by the relief workers and no toilet facilities except for one galvanised bucket for each wagon. Shortly after dawn the convoy was hitched to the train carrying the internees from the camp at Rivesaltes. At 6.40 a.m. the convoy pulled out of the station on its way north, linking up at Sorgue–Châteauneuf-du-Pape with the train from Les Milles that Ross and Lindsley had watched being loaded, before continuing on to Drancy.

Now that the deportations had begun, Mary's focus – and that of the other relief workers in the camp – had altered dramatically. For years her concerns had been primarily to feed and clothe the internees, to help re-unite families and make contact with their relatives living abroad. Now her priorities altered overnight: from now on she must save as many lives as possible, through any means available, legal or otherwise.

***

In total, nine convoys of Jews left Rivesaltes, the last departing on 19 October 1942. In all, 2,289 people were deported from the camp, including 110 children – a figure that would have undoubtedly been considerably higher had it not been for the efforts of Mary and her colleagues. Delays in the granting of visas and other bureaucratic complications meant numerous Jews were deported despite having the relevant documentation to emigrate or being just a day or two away from obtaining one. For children under sixteen, however, the situation was more hopeful. The Vichy authorities had authorised the relief agencies to remove from the camp all such children, provided that they obtained written permission from their parents. This meant that these children could be placed in colonies such as the ones Mary had used to house Spanish children from the camps constructed after the Retirada. Now the stakes were even higher.

High in the mountains close to the walled village of Mosset, Mary had discovered an isolated dwelling called La Coume. As she explained to her friend Rose Duroux in a letter written in 1999, just three years before Mary's death, the house was Quaker-owned, having been bought by the veteran relief worker Edith Pye: "We were able to send Spanish children from the camps … along the beaches there." In the summer of 1942 La Coume would prove to be an ideal location to hide Jewish children under threat of deportation. In October, Burritt Hiatt, a Quaker and businessman from Ohio, who had assumed the leadership of the Marseille office in early 1942, visited the camp of Rivesaltes to see Mary's area of operation. During this visit they both made the trip up to La Coume. His diary records a day that began high in the Pyrenees. Here he describes their arrival:

> To reach it we had to park the automobile on a mountain road and walk up a foot path for a quarter of an hour. When we approached the buildings we could see that the house was in disrepair and that the roof of the barn had fallen in. A donkey and a pig were wandering around, unrestrained by any fences.

Children in camp, unknown location.

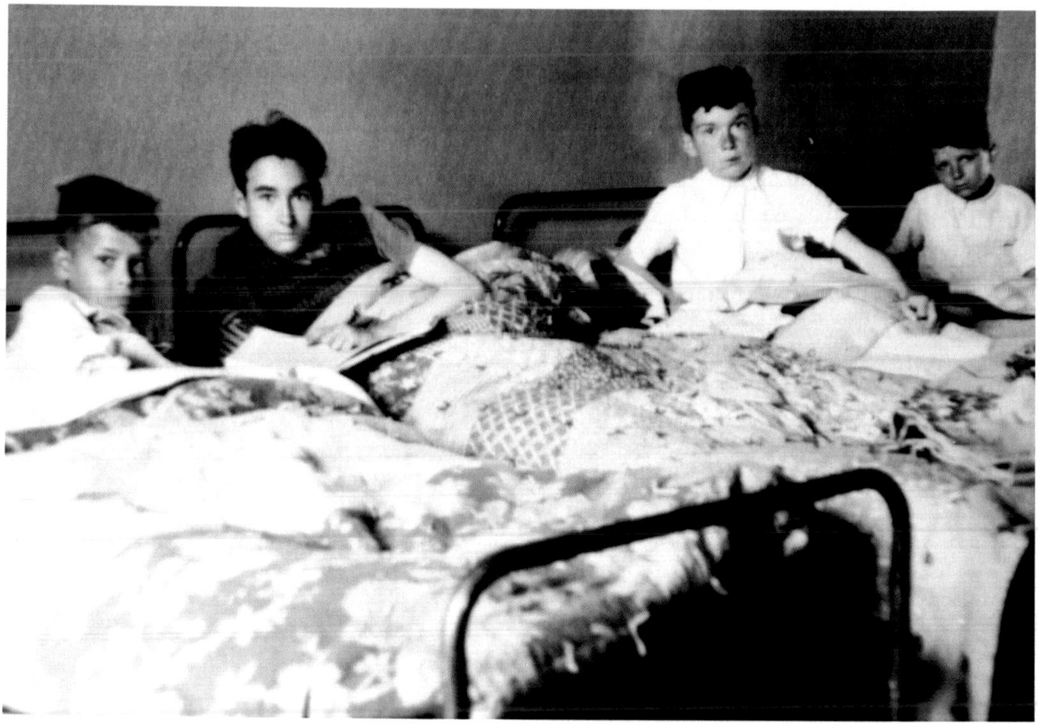
Boys' dorm in children's colony.

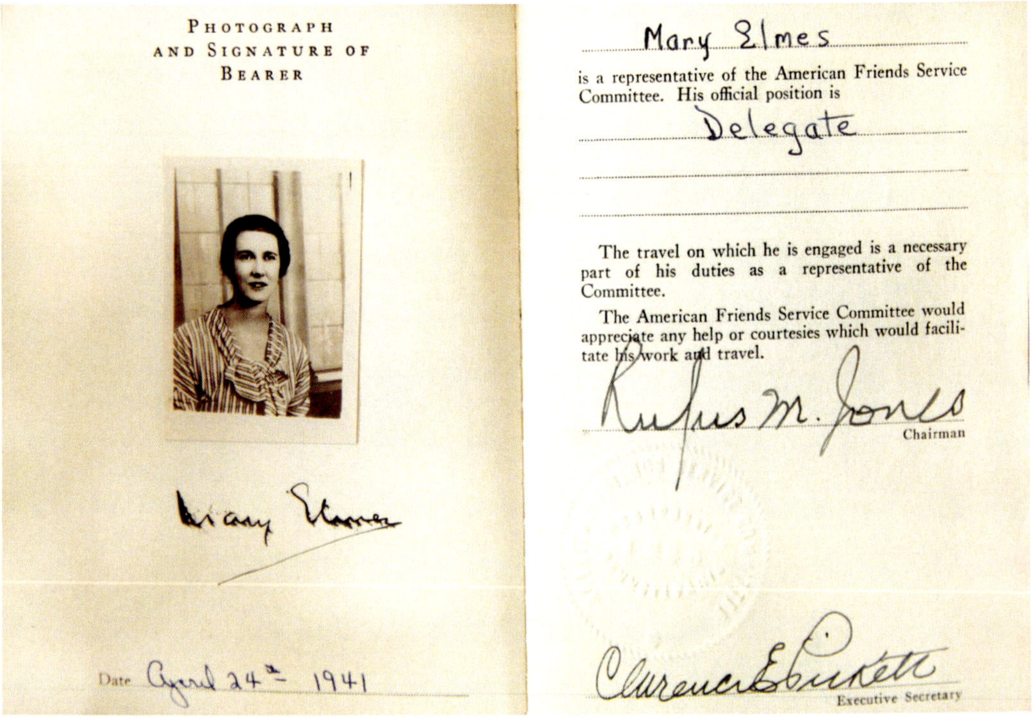

PHOTOGRAPH
AND SIGNATURE OF
BEARER

Mary Elmes

Date April 24th 1941

Mary Elmes

is a representative of the American Friends Service Committee. His official position is

Delegate

The travel on which he is engaged is a necessary part of his duties as a representative of the Committee.

The American Friends Service Committee would appreciate any help or courtesies which would facilitate his work and travel.

Rufus M. Jones
Chairman

Clarence E. Pickett
Executive Secretary

Mary's AFSC Quaker ID.

Signed photo of Pablo Casals given to Mary in 1940.

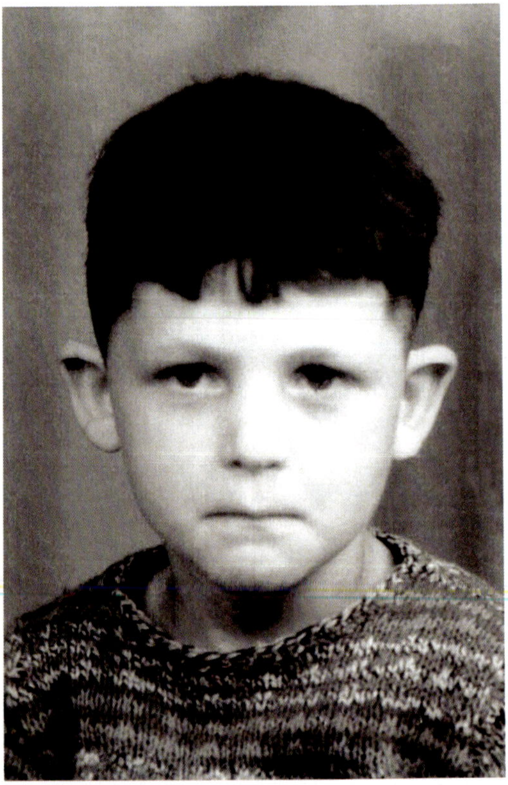

Réné Freund (Ron Friend) – taken in Britain shortly after the war.

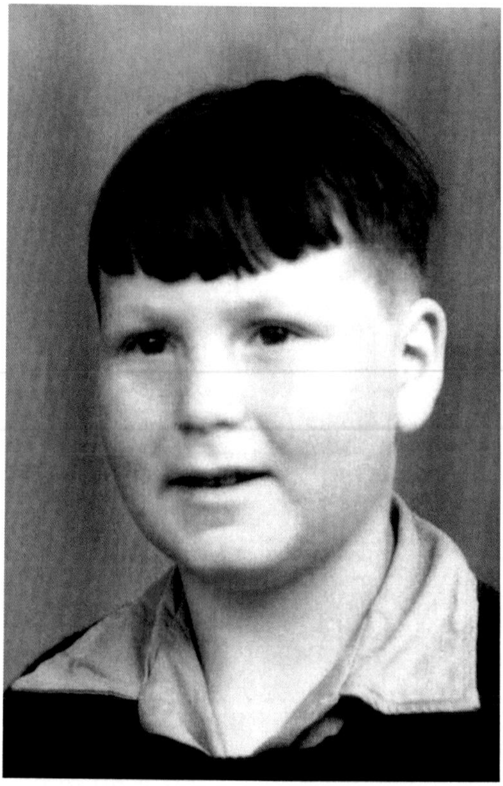

Mario (Michael) Freund – taken in Britain shortly after the war.

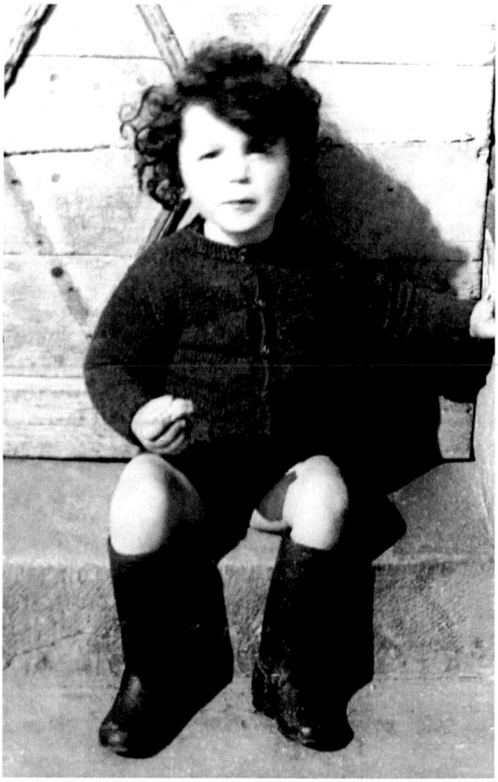

Réné Freund as a toddler in Marssac after being rescued by Mary.

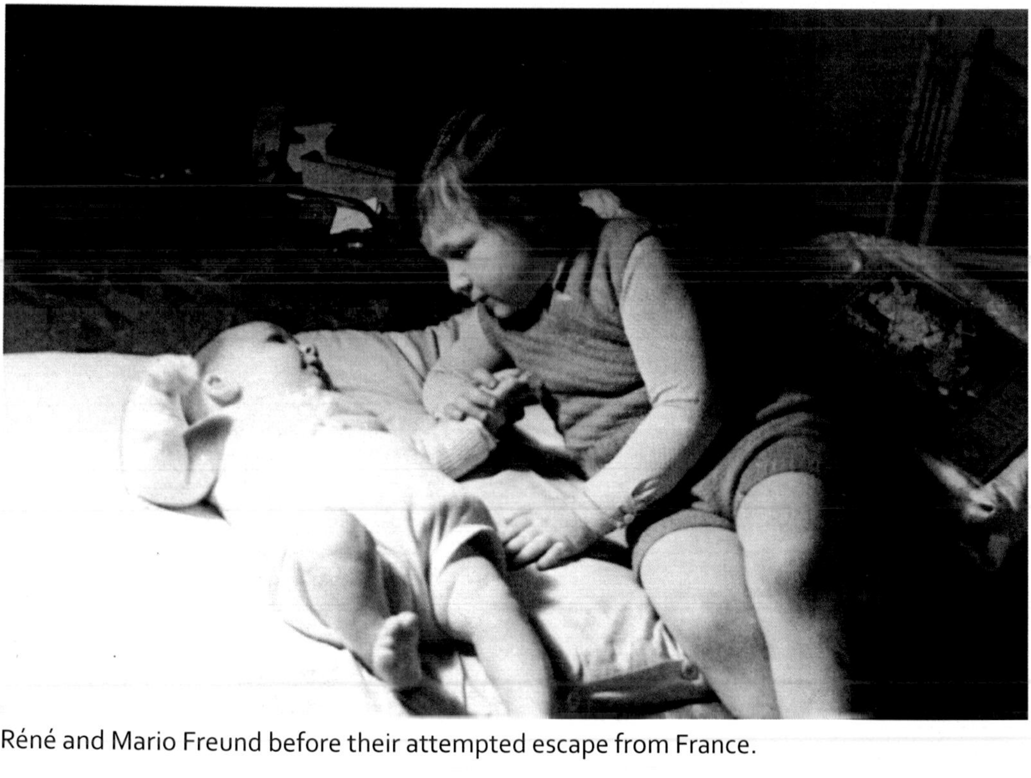

Réné and Mario Freund before their attempted escape from France.

Eva and Hans Freund.

Hans Freund.

Eva, Réné and Mario Freund with unknown woman.

Réné Freund in his aunt and uncle's house in Ilford after the war, age 6.

Mario Freund in his aunt and uncle's house in Ilford after the war, age 10.

Mary and her son, Patrick.

Friedel Bohny-Reiter presenting Mary with a watercolour of the camp at Rivesaltes.

Mary's children and great-grandchildren at the Righteous ceremony, 2014.

Barracks in Rivesaltes.

Entrance to camp at Rivesaltes.

Rail line from Rivesaltes camp to Drancy.

Unveiling of memorial stele near the site of the children's colony at Canet-la-Plage, 2014.

The pair were greeted by the director of the colony, Pitt Kreuger, and his wife, Yvès, both of whom had been teachers for pupils with special needs in Germany. The couple had fled their homeland as the Nazis rose to power and settled at La Coume, where they established their colony as a haven for all those escaping fascism. At the time of Mary and Burittt's visit there were sixteen children in the colony, including the Kreugers' two daughters. Burittt's dairy continues:

> The Kreugers hurriedly discussed with Mary Elmes the progress of each of the children. They took us into the house to the store of food that they saved for the winter.
>
> In one room a half dozen young children were seated around a kindergarten table where a young girl was teaching them. … In another room I saw shelf after shelf of books that belonged to Mr. Kreuger, a wonderful collection to have in a mountain farmhouse where there are few other distractions. …
>
> As we were leaving I saw three boys standing motionless in a shed with their backs to us. They were three brothers of the orthodox Jewish faith, who stood inactive on certain days. I was struck that such small boys, without parents or other Jews about, would observe religious rites so conscientiously.

The relief agencies were supposed to operate only within the strict legal terms set out by Vichy; otherwise they risked being barred from performing any duties in the camps at all. Like many of her colleagues, Mary simply ignored these strictures and sought to free as many people as possible. As Alice Resch, of the AFSC's Toulouse office, wrote in her memoir:

> … we worked almost daily, hiding both adults and children and securing false identity papers and ration cards. But this was all done on the sly, even among those in the office. We were a neutral, non-political organization after all, and foreigners to boot. We had to be very, very careful not to compromise our work in the camps for the French children.

Although appearing to adhere to the rules laid down by the Vichy authorities, the real intention of Mary and her colleagues was to hide Jewish children for as long as required to prevent their deportation. Initially, parents were understandably reluctant to hand over their children to the aid workers, meaning that children left on convoys with their families. As the stark reality of the deportations became clear to those awaiting transport to the east, however, Mary's arrival at the camp would be met by anguished shouts from distraught mothers, pleading in all the tongues of Europe the same desperate refrain: "Take my child, take my child." Throughout the summer the convoys continued provoking heart-rending scenes as mothers were separated from the children they were leaving behind. One such woman was a 24-year-old Polish mother called Léa Drommelschlager. On the day of her and her husband's deportation from Rivesaltes in September 1942, Léa passed on a letter for her three-year-old son, part of which read:

> My very dear only little child, I hope my few words reach you, and that you will be able to read them one day, when you are able to understand the gravity of events … you are our only thought and we are forced to leave you, to uproot you from those who are closest to you at a moment when you really need them …. I don't know if we can keep the hope that we will see you one day. If we are dead or lost, as soon as events permit, contact your grandparents for whom you will replace [their] lost children.

Some adult internees could be released if they obtained authorisation from the local prefect to live in his Department by proving that they had sufficient personal funds to support themselves. This process was a lengthy and complicated one. Once authorised by the prefecture each such application had to be passed onto Vichy's Interior Ministry for validation. The process had been further complicated by a change in the law in June 1941 which meant that only Jews who had been domiciled in France before 10 May 1940 could apply. Meanwhile, those anxiously awaiting clearance to leave Rivesaltes watched as the trains departed to the death camps. Beyond assisting people with their applications to the prefects or their visa requests there was little more Mary could do for the adult internees. The children, however, were a different matter.

On 26 August, three days after the second convoy left Rivesaltes for Auschwitz, police launched a massive round-up of Jews in the Unoccupied Zone, arresting 7,000 people. Unhappy with the numbers of those caught up in the raids, Réné Bousquet sent telegrams to all the prefects in the Unoccupied Zone urging them to redouble their efforts. All those arrested were taken to Rivesaltes. No longer would the camp masquerade as a family residential camp. From now on its function was nothing less than to act as a holding centre for Jews marked down for slaughter.

On 11 September, two young boys named Réné and Mario Freund were brought into Rivesaltes with their parents, Hans and Eva. Hans was a consultant engineer, his wife a doctor. Uneasy about the rising influence of the Nazi party, the family had left their home in Berlin in 1933, the year Hitler became German Chancellor, to move to Milan, where Hans worked as an advisor to the Fiat car company. In Milan Eva gave birth to the couple's first son, Mario. In 1938 the Freunds moved to Paris, where Hans worked as a consultant for the SNCF, the French national rail network. By an ironic twist of fate, just five years later the rolling stock of this same company would transport him and almost 80,000 fellow Jews to their deaths. In September 1939, when Eva was seven months pregnant, her husband was arrested as an 'undesirable alien' and interned in a camp at Villebon, southwest of Paris. The couple's second son, Réné, was born in October. Hans was released from Villebon in February 1940, whereupon the family moved, initially, to Albi in southern France before re-locating in December to the village of Marssac, to the northwest of Toulouse. By the summer of 1942 Hans and Eva were becoming increasingly concerned for the safety of their family and began making plans to escape over the border into Switzerland, where Hans had a number of business associates. Hans hired a car to take the family to the frontier. As his elder son recalled in an interview for the documentary *It Tolls for Thee*:

> The car stopped short of the border and we got out, my father and I were walking ahead of my mother who was carrying my

> brother. We were to meet a farmer who was carrying a sack on his back in a field but he wasn't going to approach us, we were just going to follow him. We did see the farmer and we started following him.

After what seemed like an eternity Hans and his son finally made it safely across the border, but his wife and Réné had lagged behind and were still on French territory. When Hans and Mario ventured back to help his wife and baby son the family were arrested by armed French border guards.

> And so we came back, the farmer kept on going. And at that point the police took us to the border control and my mother and father were questioned inside, my brother and I were playing around outside. It took hours. Later on we were loaded onto a vehicle and taken to Rivesaltes. I remember the building we were in. It was a long stone or brick building, just like a barn, and there were watchtowers and barbed wire everywhere.

Somehow Hans managed to get news of his family's predicament to relatives in Britain, who contacted the Quakers for help. Sometime before making the desperate attempt to flee to Switzerland Hans had contacted the AFSC office in Marseille seeking help in arranging American visas for the family. On 7 September, Mary's colleagues in Marseille wrote to Mary, advising her of the family's presence in Rivesaltes:

> This is a man with whom we have had some correspondences during the past couple of months, and for whom we cabled Philadelphia on August 7th, asking for confirmation of his visa status. There is as yet no reply, but one may arrive at any moment, and we shall forward it immediately.
>
> Would you be good enough to try to see him, tell him there is unfortunately nothing further we can do, and transmit to him all our sympathy?

Two weeks later Una Mortished in Marseille passed on to Mary the following cable from the AFSC's London office:

> SPECIAL URGENT REQUEST YOUR HELP THROUGH PERPIGNAN OFFICE ASSISTANCE CASE 88 HANS FREUND AND FAMILY ILOT K BARAQUE 35 RIVESALTES STOP.

Una's letter added: "We wonder whether the whole family is still at Rivesaltes, or whether it has been deported already. Can you investigate for us and let us know as soon as possible?"

Mary replied three days later, on 25 August 1942, confirming that the family were indeed still at Rivesaltes:

> The two children will probably be liberated this evening from the camp ... and we are sending them to [the children's colony in] Vernet [-les-Bains]. The father is anxious that the children should go to the United States in a convoy and he has signed the necessary discharges confiding the children to our care. He and his have some hope that their case can be termined [sic] favourably and send many messages of thanks to their friends who enquire about them. They are extremely anxious that every step should be taken to hasten on the granting of their American visas.

For Hans, however, as with so many others trapped in similar circumstances, the long-awaited visa would never arrive. On 4 March 1944, after he and Eva had been transferred to the camp at Gurs, Hans left Drancy on Convoy 50 to his death in the extermination camp of Majdanek in Poland. He was one of 200 Jews whom the German authorities had insisted be deported in reprisal for the shooting dead in Paris of two Luftwaffe officers by members of the French Resistance.

The same day as the transport left Les Milles, Mary wrote to Andrée Montagnon in Marseille, hinting of her frustration at trying against all odds to help those in the camp and the emotional impact it had on her and her colleagues when their efforts proved fruitless:

> Thank you for your letter of August 7th. I was glad to see the person whom you introduced by this letter, but I regret very much that there was nothing that I could do to help him.
>
> I have frequently explained in Marseille that we are not equipped here to help such cases and have asked specifically that they should not be addressed to us, as we have the painful task of having to refuse such help.

By the end of August 1942 the camp at Rivesaltes had become the main holding camp for all Jews arrested in the Unoccupied Zone, operating under the title of Centre National de Rassemblement des Israélites. The status of children who were exempted from the transports, constantly liable to change, was becoming increasingly precarious. On 26 September, Mary, having obtained the necessary permission from their parents, moved to liberate Mario and Réné before it was too late. It is highly unlikely that she possessed the required medical attestation from the camp doctor certifying that the brothers were medically fit to leave the camp since both children were suffering from a severe outbreak of scabies picked up in their filthy barrack. Nevertheless, Mary, most likely with a nod from Captain Humbert, succeeded in having them officially released and drove them herself to the children's colony high up at the Hotel du Portugal at Vernet-les-Bains. When the exhausted children finally reached the hotel the resident doctor there refused to allow them to sleep in the same rooms as the other children, for fear their scabies would infect the whole colony. Mary spent the night with the brothers in hastily arranged isolated sleeping quarters. The following morning she drove them to St Louis Hospital in Perpignan. While Mario and Réné were being treated in the hospital, Mary was arranging the next step in their journey to safety. The brothers were released from St Louis on 14 November, two days before their parents were transferred from Rivesaltes to the camp at Gurs, and spirited away to a safe house in Toulouse. From there Mary had arranged for Father Louis Bézard, the curé from Marssac-sur-Tarn, a village located 70 kilometres north of Toulouse, to take the boys and hide them in his presbytery. Curé Bézard and his helper, André Voilier, duly collected the brothers from their safe house in Toulouse. A short while later, at the city's train station, disaster struck when the group walked straight into a Gestapo raid. In an account of the episode written by the curé in the 1950s, he explained how they avoided arrest as the Gestapo made their way along the platform checking identity papers and taking away those whose documents were not in order. André and the curé calmly gestured to Mario and Réné to hide between the two suitcases the men were carrying before Father Bézard draped his coat over the luggage. The ruse worked. The immediate danger had passed, leaving the little group free to continue their journey to Marssac. Two days before Réné and Mario were released from hospital a pastoral letter from Jules-Géraud Saliège, Archbishop of Toulouse, was read out in all churches in the region. This move marked a significant change in official Catholic Church attitudes, which up to this point had been supportive of Vichy and its commitment to traditional values, and reflected a new mood among the public prompted by the deportation of children. The letter pointed out that:

> The treatment of children, women, fathers, and mothers like herds of cattle, the separation of members of the family from one another and their deportation to unknown destinations, are sad spectacles which have been reserved for us to witness in our times. Why does the church's right of Asylum no longer exist? Why are we defeated? Lord have mercy on us. ... Jews are men and women. They are all brothers. A Christian cannot forget that.

Three days later, the Bishop of Montauban, Pierre-Marie Théas, followed with a letter of his own condemning the Government's anti-Semitic measures.

***

The unbearable reality of the deportations is sharply evoked in Friedel Bohny-Reiter's diary entry for 19 August:

> The moans of tormented people again floating on the air. I see them in long lines from their barracks, panting from the weight of their possessions. The guards at their sides. Being put into ranks for roll-call. Waiting for hours in a field exposed to the sun. Then the lorries arrive to take them to the railway lines. They get out of the lorries flanked by two rows of guards and get into cattle wagons, some of them hesitant, others apathetic, some with a defiant air, their heads held high. This goes on for hours until they are all crammed into the stiflingly hot wagons.

For historian Denis Peschanski, each transport involved a series of ordeals for those involved:

> Each deportation was an extremely traumatic experience. The first stage was the screening process. A [screening] committee in the Rivesaltes camp had to say who is being sent away and who is being kept. The second traumatic moment was when they were rounded up in the camp and put into wagons. The only photographs we have of Jews being herded together in a camp before their deportation are photographs taken [clandestinely by Friedel Bohny-Reiter] at Rivesaltes, which are extremely moving. The third trauma was the journey, because it took two or three days to go from Rivesaltes to Drancy. It was absolute horror and perhaps the most terrible moment was when the children were deported.

He points out that in the summer of 1942, in the initial phase of the deportations, the German authorities were targeting only adults over sixteen.

> And then from Laval came a request to deport children from the southern [Vichy] zone. The request was sent to Berlin but before the order came back the parents were deported and the children had been left behind .... We see children arriving at Drancy all alone. Completely lost – 3,500 of them. They were then deported

> in horrible conditions – an absolute tragedy. For me that is the symbol of the Final Solution, the desire to destroy people, right down to children, even babies. They wanted to make a whole people disappear. That's what the Final Solution was.

On the question of who really understood the reality of the deportations, journalist John Baskin believes relief workers such as Mary were the first people to realise the true nature of what was going on in Eastern Europe:

> No one was putting the picture together because no one could believe that a part of humanity could behave this way. Mary and the others began to see that it was so deep: if the Jews didn't know what was happening to them why were they killing themselves when the train came? They knew what was happening in the camps. If it was that bad here what would it be like on the other end? And also it didn't make sense; they were taking the aged, the infirm, people with palsy, people who were bed-ridden and saying 'you're going to the east and you will work'. Children, small children. It didn't make any sense to those sort of veterans like Mary. They didn't believe it for a minute … they were really part of the first vanguard who really understood what was going on. The rest of the world was still dithering.

For many of the relief workers the deportations posed a moral dilemma. Many questioned their own involvement, asking themselves whether, by distributing food and water to those on the trains, they were tacitly abetting the French police. Denis Peschanski poses the question that many relief workers had been forced to confront:

> Are you complicit in the deportations just by being there? Do you say 'no' and refuse to intervene? It's terrible because if you say 'no', everyone goes away. If you say 'yes' you can save some of them. It goes even further …. At one time under pressure from the French police people would say to them: 'Okay, you have hidden fifty of

> them, but I've got to fill the convoy so go and find fifty others.' And a few days later the fifty that were hidden, they are all also deported. You can imagine what a terrible situation it was for the aid agencies if they decided to stay strictly legal. If you add it up, it was a very difficult situation but it is clear that they were able to save more people than if they hadn't intervened.

Nazi hunter Efraim Zuroff offers his view about the choices Mary and her colleagues faced:

> I understand the moral dilemma but they [the relief workers] had a unique opportunity to help people who ultimately were designated to be murdered. And the question is what do you do in that situation? Do you say: 'I just want to stay around and help the people who are left or do I actively try to extricate people from these camps whose fate is basically sealed?' It reminds me of the whole issue of the legality of the measures taken by the Germans. Every measure they took was legal because according to the laws of the Third Reich those measures were fine, they were within the law. But clearly we're talking about measures that were intrinsically illegal and under those conditions one would hope that people had the brains and moral integrity to understand that these laws should be broken. Unfortunately not everyone is that type of person.

Conscious of the strain Mary was enduring as the deportations continued, her colleague Russell Ritchie in Marseille wrote to her on 14 August to offer what support he could: "We have a great deal of sympathy for the sad burden you've been carrying just recently. It's a rotten business."

Mary and her colleagues in the other aid agencies had stepped up their effort to get Jewish children out of the camp into the relative safety of the colonies or to facilitate their emigration to the United States. Vivette Samuel, of the OSE, has written that in June 1942 only five [Jewish] children, whose parents could not bear to be separated from them, were left in the camp.

On 7 August, the delegates of the various relief agencies were called together by the camp administration for a meeting with members of the Perpignan Prefecture in charge of deciding which internees were to be deported. As Andrée Salomon of L'Oeuvre de Secours aux Enfants (OSE) recounted, the visitors brought devastating news: from now on children would be included in the deportations. Andrée later wrote:

> The children had to be taken out of the camp at all costs. Miss Elms [sic], the Quaker delegate, immediately took a first group with her in her own car and came back the same day in search of the rest. The camp administration agreed to validate this departure as a regular liberation. Hence, not a single Jewish child remained in the camp.

By the end of the month new Jewish families caught up in the round-ups planned for the Unoccupied Zone would find themselves herded into Block K to await their fate.

In mid-September Ross McClelland travelled from Marseille to Rivesaltes to see for himself conditions in the camp:

> After I had received the permit from the commandant, I went to the room in one of the barracks where Miss Elmes interviews a succession of persons who come to her for help. It was not possible to detail the subject matter of all these interviews, but I shall use one or two for illustration. A Belgian doctor of science who once had charge of an orphanage came in to ask if he would be eligible as an escort for children [being sent] to America. He was a proficient looking man in the prime of life and seemed confident that he would not be included in future convoys. This illustrates one of the difficulties under which Miss Elmes must work, because she had confidential advice which she could not communicate to him that he would be in the group leaving the following Tuesday. In addition to asking consideration for himself, this Belgian doctor said that there were several old people in the same building as himself who had endemia for several days. They could not recover

> on the rough diet of the camp. He demanded that the Quakers send these people some supplementary food which would aid their recovery. Some of the refugees feel that the Quakers are in possession of an inexhaustible supply of food which we have no right to refuse giving to people who are ill.

In October, Burritt Hiatt, the new leader of the Marseille office, visited the camp of Rivesaltes and had dinner with Mary at her apartment. His journal makes clear that she obviously made a strong impression on him:

> Miss Mary Elmes moves about quietly and unostentatiously. A simple character, but firm. She is sensitive to art, as her apartment shows, and prefers the Spanish motif .... During our conversation I tried to get from her a picture of her day as a relief worker. Of course her main effort has been in camp Rivesaltes, where she has succeeded in getting many people exempted from the deportations northward. In addition, she has supervised the feeding of children in the camp, given supplementary food to men in the camp hospital, conducted a self-help workshop there and consulted the internees regarding their emigration. Outside the camp she supervised for children's residence colonies and also supervised the care of a dozen children in their own homes. She has the supervision of medical equipment for refugees such as belts, orthopaedic limbs, glasses, false teeth, etc. She contacts the prefecture for cards of identity, for permissions and visas for liberated refugees. She runs a work-room for women, a distribution of clothing, and a distribution of milk for children. In addition, she supervises relief work in some neighbouring towns such as Narbonne, Montpellier, etc.

Mary obviously took the opportunity to voice her misgivings about her relationship with colleagues in Marseille:

> Mary Elmes feels out of touch with the home office in Marseille. ... In the first place, she feels that important decisions affecting

> her work are not sent to her rapidly enough for her to adapt her program to them. Sometimes it is only out in the field that she runs into a decision that has been made. In the second place, when she makes proposals to the home office in Marseille she has difficulty in learning what has become of her suggestions.

On the second day of Burritt Hiatt's visit Mary drove him to the children's colony at Canet-le-Plage. The journal continues:

> I had expected it to be on a point overlooking the sea but it was on the low sandy ground and the old three-story building was like a barrack. We watched the forty-nine children at their luncheon of beans, greens and bread which was carefully weighed to them in proportion to their age. After lunch the children went out into the courtyard because the sun there was warmer than in the house. They were not active – merely seeking warmth.

Burritt found his visit disappointing:

> I was not as impressed with colony life as I had expected. The children seem to have so few possessions of their own or interests of their own. Even a poor [family] home gives loyalties and something distinctly their own.

Next stop was a visit to a former convent, which had been turned into a hospital. Conditions there were grim:

> It had no heat, no plumbing and no furniture. The men lay on pallets on the floor. The medical attention was by refugee doctors and amateur nurses. The equipment for disinfecting instruments was primitive. The Quakers provide a supplementary food for the men who are not thriving on the regular diet. They were designated by red cards above their beds. Mary Elmes passed through the long rows of pallets and the faces of the men lighted up as she had a word for them.

> She gave a letter to one man from his wife in England from whom he had not heard for months. She promised a book to this one and made a note to bring something to the next one. With many pauses by bedsides we passed through a half dozen wards. In the last ward were twenty tubercular men. … One young fellow lay there with his cheeks flushed and his eyes glistening. Next to him a huge, gaunt man formed a smile with his lips. A Spaniard, who had contracted tuberculosis during imprisonment, wished to speak something to Miss Elmes in his language. At the exit a middle-aged man rose to his feet and waited to be recognised. He had been carried into the hospital a few weeks before, paralysed from the deficiency of the diet in the internment camp. Mary Elmes had supplied some beef supplements which had enabled him to stand now and take a few steps.
>
> Outside in the open air an Alsatian doctor stopped me to inquire what preparations America was making to relieve such a situation. The whole impersonal process by which racial and national discrimination brings men to such a place strikes one as monstrous beyond words.
>
> The presence there of a woman like Mary Elmes is a fragment from another world – an influence and partly an inspiration.

After Mary had seen to some business with the local prefect – whom the journal describes as having greeted her warmly and spoken to her as he would to an intimate – Mary and Burritt drove to Rivesaltes.

> We went through openings in barbed-wire fences guided by soldiers and finally pulled up at one of the low buildings which was the office of the Commandant. We waited on the bench outside the door for a few moments in the strained atmosphere of anxious people and over-driven clerks. It was a place where decisions of life and death were made in the preparation of deportation lists.

They then proceeded to Mary's office, where a large number of people were waiting to see her:

> … many of them so confused by anxiety that it required patience for her to unravel their stories. One man who was bandaged had been beaten by the guards, another had been classified under the wrong nationality, another wished to be transferred to a work company to be near his invalid wife.
>
> Through the door of the room where we were sitting I could see some of the internees walking back and forth between the barracks. Some were quite advanced in years – professional people now reduced to spending their days pre-occupied with hunger and cold. Their only possessions were those that could be kept under a pallet on the floor. We visited some of these buildings to interview people who could not come to Miss Elmes' offices. For them she took telegrams or inspected papers or wrote prescriptions for food or medicine.
>
> We left this depressing camp at sundown. Queues of people were waiting in line for food for the evening meal. Then they would return to their quarters where there was no privacy and bed down for another dreary night. Perhaps glad to be spared another day from deportation.

During Burritt's visit Mary had explained how difficult she found it to keep track of people in the camp because they were moved so often from one barrack to another. This wasted a lot of her time, she said, adding that frequently those who needed her help the most were the most timid about finding her. She also confided how emotionally draining she found it to interview people who she already knew were due to deported but who themselves did not and whom it was beyond her power to help.

The following day Mary drove Burritt to the colony in Vernet-les-Bains high up in the Pyrenees, where he wrote:

> I am in a room in the children's colony …. Outside the window runs a swift mountain stream. Sleeping in other parts of this house tonight are forty-four Spanish children – some of them as young as four years. Fourteen of them have no parents. Another fourteen have a mother but she is either in the internment camp,

> in the hospital or working at a job where her wages are not sufficient to take her child. The remaining sixteen have parents who can give something towards their support.
>
> Mary Elmes and I arrived here last evening just as the children were having their afternoon taste of hot milk at the tables under the trees. When the children spied Mary Elmes they cried 'Maria' and rushed to her. Some of the older girls of fourteen or fifteen were helping the smaller children with their food. Some of them seemed almost babies as they had to be helped up and down from the benches. … Mary seemed to be familiar with the name and background of each child.

A week after Burritt returned to Marseille, on 20 October 1942, the final convoy of 107 people left Rivesaltes for Drancy. Although the last train had headed northwards, Mary's work was far from over. On 11 November 1942 Germany invaded the Unoccupied Zone in response to the Allied landings in North Africa. The remaining internees were transferred from Rivesaltes to Gurs. By the end of the month the camp was being used to billet German troops of the 7th Panzer Division, whose orders were to defend the south coast from an Allied landing. No longer could Mary rely for help on the sympathetic Captain Humbert or the mayors and prefects she had built such close working links with. Early in the New Year the woman who had done so much to save others would find herself alone against the might of the Nazi invaders.

Unknown to Mary, the surveillance operation directed towards her had been enhanced in the weeks following a tip-off to police by the woman who denounced her. Dark forces were closing in on Mary, but still she strove to help those in desperate need. On 3 February 1943 the Gestapo made their move. Now the woman who had helped liberate so many others was herself a captive, facing deportation to the death camps, where so many people from Rivesaltes, whose names and history she knew and whose futures she had laboured so hard to safeguard, had already perished.

7

Arrest

After her arrest Mary's Gestapo captors drove her the short distance to Perpignan prison, where she was put in a cell for the night pending her transfer to the military prison in Toulouse, 200 kilometres to the north. For decades she remained silent on the circumstances that had led to her imprisonment, but during an interview in old age she revealed that her informer was the wife of a guard at Rivesaltes:

> I was arrested because [she] was apparently jealous. We distributed things to people in the camps and not to her … so she made a false declaration … she was the wife of one of the guards in the camp … that's all I know about her, all that I want to know. For a long time I didn't want to know anything about it … I was afraid I was suspecting something that was quite innocent.

Despite being accused of providing Jews with forged papers and helping their escape from France, she was never officially charged with any offence. Nevertheless she spent six months behind bars and watched helplessly as some of her fellow prisoners were tortured and deported to the death camps in Eastern Europe.

The day after her arrest, as most of the city still slept, Mary was taken from her cell and taken to St Michel Prison in Toulouse. This gloomy redbrick building, built in the style of a medieval château with castellated walls and turrets, looms over its *quartier*, not far from the Canal du Midi. At the time of Mary's arrest the prison was under SS control. Many of those held there were *résistants*, one of whom was the acclaimed French author André Malraux. Mary was held here for three months and recalled that the jail was "full of bums [ordinary criminals] and things like that and we didn't have much to eat." She remained in the military prison until 31 March, when she was transferred by train to the notorious Fresnes Prison in Paris.

The news of Mary's imprisonment sparked shock and alarm among her colleagues, who lost no time in challenging the grounds for her arrest and demanding her release. On the day of her arrest, Professor Lucien Cornil of Secours Quaker[§] wrote in French to Seán Murphy, the Irish delegate in Vichy, urging him to contact the 'occupying authorities', noting that:

> It seems that this arrest happened, not through her being our representative but for personal reasons ....
>
> Mary Elmes, whose devotion, nobility of spirit and profound selflessness are well known to her entourage, has achieved over many years a labour of active generosity beyond all praise. From knowing her personally I cannot think that she is in any way compromised in carrying out this work.

Professor Cornil concluded by pointing out that "the Germans in Paris and Toulouse recognise that our work is strictly limited to acts of charity." Some months later he again wrote:

> Miss Mary Elmes is one of the Quakers' longest serving workers and has been head of the Delegation in Perpignon since the summer of 1940.
>
> An excellent organiser, she has always worked with great devotion, without regard to her health – still quite fragile – in a spirit of great objectivity, available to [treat] all human suffering and according to the Quaker tradition without taking sides and eschewing all politics.

[§] In December 1942, the American Friends Service Committee (AFSC) became known as Secours Quakers.

> She is held in esteem and loved by her entourage. Her prolonged absence is seriously hindering the good functioning of the services provided by the delegation [children's colonies, school canteens, food and clothes distribution, etc. ...]

On hearing of Mary's arrest, Helga Holbek, the Quakers' Toulouse delegate, and a colleague immediately made their way to the local prefecture to attempt to secure Mary's release. There they were told in no uncertain terms that nothing could be done because her arrest was now a matter for the German authorities. Undaunted, the two women continued on to 2 rue de Maignan, then the Toulouse headquarters of the Gestapo, where their efforts to have their colleague released proved equally fruitless, although they did secure permission to visit Mary and to send her a package containing food and other necessities. Meanwhile, the AFSC hierarchy used its high-level international connections to maximise its influence on Mary's behalf.

In Cork, Mary's mother was unwell at the time, prompting Secours Quakers to contact her brother, John, with the news of his sister's detention. John made the decision to conceal word of Mary's predicament from his mother, hoping that his sister – as an aid worker and a neutral – would soon be released. Such hopes were to prove unfounded in the short-term but, ironically, it was Mary's mother who would ultimately play a key role in her release.

Perhaps sensing that something was amiss, Mrs Elmes wrote to the AFSC in March, anxiously seeking news of her daughter, still unaware that she had been imprisoned:

> I have heard nothing from her since November 11, 1942 when she called and have no means of knowing if she gets my weekend letters. ... I have protested several times to the Irish Department of Foreign Affairs of this lack of facilities for correspondence. She is a neutral working in a foreign country and should be allowed to correspond with her home people.

On 17 March Hélene Rott de Noufville, a member of the Toulouse delegation, made contact with Roger Danjou, a native of Normandy who specialised in forestry management, with news of her situation (Roger was dating Mary and the pair would marry in 1946): "After asking for special authorisation I was able to bring your package to your friend last Saturday. I have just heard this morning that the package has been given to her and it's given her great pleasure." Her letter went on to say that a representative of the Red Cross had seen Mary and reported that she was in good health. Two days later Hélene wrote to Roger again, this time arranging for him to visit a Madame Markewich (possibly of the Red Cross), who had permission to visit Mary in prison in Toulouse and wanted to update him on her situation. Hélene herself had some news to impart:

> Yesterday we had a visit from someone who left the PM [military prison] and who told us that Mary is doing well, in good spirits and is hoping something will be done to have her released.
>
> She has received your package. Today I'll only send her some milk and biscuits so that I'll be able to pass on the [new] package that you're going to bring.

Mary had been able to write to her colleagues asking for extra food to be sent to her. In reply, Mlle Lliboutry at the Perpignan delegation wrote to a colleague:

> We've sent as arranged two parcels to Marie [sic] containing: milk, sardines … cakes, sugar, etc. … and two parcels of fruit.
>
> In addition we sent a summer dress and espadrilles and are thinking of sending her another one. …

When Mary's mother finally discovered her daughter was in prison she wrote to Margaret Frawley of the AFSC in the United States on 18 June:

> It was on Tuesday, June 15 that I heard from Miss Emily Hughes, Friends House [in London] that Mary was under arrest and in Fresnes Prison, Paris. It came as a dreadful shock. …

> It appears that my son has known since February 24, when the Department of External Affairs telephoned that they had this news. … But my doctor would not allow me to be told as he thought the months of anxiety would be a strain on my health. … I think a mistake has been made as one or two more things could have been done had I not been kept in ignorance.

While AFSC delegations based in Europe coordinated a series of protests to the German authorities, the US delegations also joined efforts to have Mary released. James G. Vail, secretary of the AFSC's Foreign Service Section, wrote to Irish diplomat Robert Brennan in Washington on 7 May:

> We understand that no one has been allowed to visit her or to send her food; and we do not know the charge against her, though it is perhaps fair to assume that her interest in relief work for Spanish Republican refugees may be the cause.
>
> For the whole time of her service with us, Mary Elmes has faithfully, intelligently and with signal devotion to humanity in distress administered relief to persons interned in the camps in the south western corner of France and in the hospital of St Louis in Perpignan. She has kept her affairs in scrupulous order and has done a humanitarian work which commands our unqualified respect and admiration.
>
> The matter will no doubt have been called to the attention of the Minister from Eire in Lisbon.

The Quakers were obviously anxious to arrange for Mary to leave France altogether, as the letter goes on: "We understand from Mr Nunan [of the Irish delegation in Washington] that you have a legation in Vichy and that you will be willing to communicate to your government the request that steps be taken to obtain the release of Mary Elmes to travel either to Switzerland or Portugal, where we shall be glad to be responsible for her maintenance."

Dr Frederick P. Keppel, President of the War Relief Control Board (which had been set up by President Roosevelt to vet organisations raising funds in the United States to help refugees in Europe adversely affected by the war), was Mary's mother's brother-in-law. On 28 May Margaret Frawley wrote to Mary's brother John to confirm that the AFSC had made contact with Dr Keppel:

> We have also been in touch with the Irish minister both in Washington and in Lisbon and have requested the International Red Cross to give Mary assistance with packages and other services that can be provided since as a relief worker, she is entitled to come under their care.
>
> I need not tell you how deeply distressed we have all been and that we look forward to news of her release. May I add that I worked with Mary in France in 1940 and had a very deep affection for her and know the devotion which she had doing a most difficult task.

In a memo written on 5 May to James G. Vail, Margaret Frawley notes that the AFSC was seeking to involve the International Red Cross in its efforts on Mary's behalf:

> … in January when Mary Elmes was arrested, our representatives in France asked [for] the intervention of the Irish Minister in Vichy … we have today cabled to Lisbon as follows: 'request intervention International Red Cross and Irish Minister Lisbon on behalf Mary Elmes, trusted Quaker relief worker since 1938 stop …'.

Margaret passed this news on to Dr Keppel the following day:

> We have had another letter from our representatives dated March 31 and given the enclosed report about Mary Elmes. Since Philip Conard's [of the Lisbon delegation] boat has again been delayed,

> we did not feel that we could wait for him to get back … and have accordingly cabled all their Lisbon representatives as to the intervention of the International Red Cross and the Irish Minister in Lisbon. In asking [for] this intervention, we explained that Mary has been doing relief work with us since 1938 as a relief worker. She has a status which will permit the International Red Cross to act on her behalf. James G Vail is in Washington today and plans to discuss the matter with the Irish Minister. It may be that the Irish Minister in Vichy has already done all that is possible. We are inclined to feel that some outside pressure might be more effective at this time. A week ago, I had a letter from Mrs Elmes who had not heard from Mary since November. I suggested that she write to Lisbon …. I did not tell Mrs Elmes about Mary's imprisonment but I am wondering now whether we have the right to withhold this information from her ….

On May 18 Seán Nunan wrote to James G Vail:

> … concerning the arrest and imprisonment of Mary Elmes, I have now received a reply on the matter from my Department.
>
> They inform me that they are already aware of this case and that everything possible is being done for Miss Elmes. A representative of your organisation has been in contact with our Legation in Berlin … and arrangements have been made to enable Miss Elmes to receive food parcels from the organisation.

On April 29 Margaret Frawley again wrote to Dr Keppel with details of a letter:

> … which has come from our Geneva correspondent and with reference to Mary Elmes. The full quotation relating to Mary reads as follows:
>
> 'All mail from France now takes at least two weeks and in general we hear very little. The most disquieting news has been about Mary Elmes who was apparently taken into custody by

> the occupying authorities, as Eleanor described it, for personal reasons rather than anything to do with the Committee. Apparently it was a question of having spoken of certain matters in a censored article. M. Camois of our Marseille office immediately went to Perpignan and Ima Lieven hit out for Vichy to see the Irish Minister. Since mid-February we have had no further word, but hope that matters will be straightened out, since Mary is worth her weight in gold and we hate to think of the Perpignan Delegation without her. Mary and I had hoped that perhaps she could come to Switzerland for a short vacation this Spring … (I think we would have no trouble in getting her a visa, if she could ever secure the French exit) for a much needed rest and talks with us.'
>
> (Eleanor Cohu, mentioned in this excerpt is a vice-chairman with Secours Quakers, the French committee; Mr Camois is a French businessman who is directing the work. Ima Lieven is Princess Seraphina … Lieven, a Latvian refugee who has been on the committee for several years).

By mid-July Margaret Frawley felt that the campaign to have Mary freed was moving in the right direction and replied to her mother in optimistic terms:

> Your letter of July 18 has just come and gives more hope of some action that will help Mary than any news that we have had for a long while.
>
> As I wrote you earlier our first news had been that Mary had been temporarily detained, and it was only later, after I had suggested you forward mail through Lisbon that I learned that not only was she still held but that none of our people in France had been able to help her or communicate with her. The Quaker offices, both in Geneva and Lisbon, have been most active and it was the Geneva office which first communicated with the Irish representatives in Berlin. It was also through this office and our own direct intervention with the International Red Cross that we were able finally to locate her at Fresnes.

> We have shared the news of Mary's detention with a few of her friends here, who also have the great pleasure of working with her. On their behalf, I want to say that we will continue to explore every way to obtain her release, not merely as a Quaker worker but because she has been our associate and friend. One of our hopes has been that if we could get effective intervention by the International Red Cross we could secure her release since she is entitled to certain protection and has status under the Geneva Convention as a relief worker.
>
> I am sincerely sorry that we followed the recommendation of communicating with your son in the first place instead of writing directly to you, but hope that you will feel that we have continued to leave no way unexplored which might give help to Mary. You will be interested to know that Roswell and Marjorie McClelland, our representatives in Geneva, who have been greatly concerned about Mary, know her very well, and worked with her for a year in France.

On 23 July 1943 the six-month long campaign for Mary's release finally bore fruit when she was unexpectedly set free. Her colleagues' relief at the news was, however, tempered by concerns over her future welfare, rightly suspecting that she would be closely watched by the intelligence services and might even be at risk of being re-arrested. In view of that possibility, Mary's colleagues decided that the safest course of action might be to extract her from France altogether and locate her in a neutral country. Accordingly, James G. Vail wrote to Seán Nunan at the Irish legation in Washington on 28 September to point out that he and his colleagues wished Mary to know that the AFSC would be glad to have her come to work in its Geneva office. He was obviously wary of transmitting this news by the usual means and suggested that:

> Should it be possible for such a message to be conveyed to her through neutral diplomatic channels, we would also be glad to have her know how much we appreciate her devoted service.

> Even if Miss Elmes should decide to leave France, we realise that the necessary permissions may be difficult to obtain but we should feel much easier in mind if she could be once again on neutral soil.

While no doubt appreciating her colleagues' concern for her safety and their offers to relocate her, Mary had no intention of leaving France. As ever, her sole concern was the welfare of the refugees who had had no contact with 'Miss Mary' during the six months of her imprisonment.

News of Mary's release quickly spread through her network of AFSC colleagues. A delighted Margaret Frawley wrote to Mary's mother:

> The news of Mary's release reached me while I was on holiday, and I think I do not need to tell you that such good news made it a much more pleasant holiday.
>
> We have felt here that we would be more comfortable if Mary would be willing to come out [of France] and through the Irish Legation in Washington we have sent word that we would welcome her services in either our Geneva or our Lisbon office. I am not sure we can persuade her to leave, but she might be willing to change her job to either Switzerland or Portugal, where I feel she would be much safer. I cannot tell you how relieved I am to know that she is free.

Margaret included her condolences over the recent death of Dr Keppel, adding that: "I hope that if there are any services which we can render you will feel free to call on us and will not feel that your American contacts are broken."

A short later Margaret wrote again: "It is like her to go back to Perpignan, and we can't persuade her to come out if she has made up her mind. I should still welcome her in the United States and will try to get word to her." She went on to assure Mrs Elmes that Philip Conard in Lisbon would be glad to forward her letters to her daughter, adding the proviso that: "… it would be wise to be very cautious in their content, as Mary may still be under scrutiny."

On 23 September 1943 Seán Nunan wrote an update to James G. Vail:

> With reference to previous correspondence concerning the case of Miss Mary Elmes, I have now been informed by my Department that she was released from detention on the afternoon of Friday, 23rd July. You may be interested in having the particulars of her case, as reported to me, which are as follows: '…the Department of External Affairs, Dublin were first informed of Miss Elmes' arrest by the Legation at Vichy on 18 February. The Legation stated that she had been arrested on 5 February and that they had made representations to the German authorities. On receipt of this message the [Irish] Legation at Berlin were instructed to make an immediate demarche to the German authorities and to endeavour to secure Miss Elmes' immediate release. Strong representations were made by the Legation in Berlin to the German authorities, with the result that, finally, permission was granted to a member of the Legation staff at Vichy to visit Mary Elmes, who had been transferred to Fresnes Prison, Paris, in May. The Legation at Vichy were requested to arrange a visit as soon as possible and on 26 July they reported that the secretary of the Legation had seen Mary Elmes and the officer in charge of the case at the German police headquarters, Paris, on Friday morning 23rd July. Miss Elmes was released that afternoon. She was quite well and intended to return to Perpignan in the near future to resume her work with the Friends Service Committee.'

The day after her release Mary visited the Quakers' office in Paris where she penned a letter to Helga Holbek in Toulouse:

> I am very happy and I would like first of all to thank you for all the steps you've taken for me and which have now been crowned with success.
>
> I don't know how to thank you for the magnificent parcels that you sent me when I was in Toulouse and for all the good things that you sent to the Quakers in Paris for the parcels which they

> so loyally brought to me every week. It's because of that that I'm still in such good health – otherwise I would be much more tired than I am ….
>
> I am staying a few more days in Paris while I wait for my new identity card to be delivered. Then I'll return to Perpignan to get my things and have a rest. I'm really very tired and have no strength after this long period without getting enough air.
>
> Roger Danjou told me that my ration card is in Toulouse. In that case, please send it to me urgently because I am without [food] tickets – except a few that I borrowed from him but which are insufficient for the length of my stay in Paris. I would also like to change the card and the tickets for August (they need to be sent as well) because the doctor gave me a certificate … for extra food for three months, and I'd like to take advantage of this as quickly as possible.

In another letter to her colleagues in Perpignan she wrote: "Thank you very much for all your lovely letters. They gave me a lot of pleasure. The date of my return hasn't been finalised yet. … In the end I didn't go to Normandy for a variety [of] reasons" and went on to ask if anyone could recommend somewhere for her to spend a restful few days:

> I could go to Vernet but there I would be immersed in an atmosphere of work and the preoccupations of Secour Quakers and I would prefer to be well away from these worries during my little holiday. … I would like to find a place where I had a bit of company because a stay in a hotel all alone can be a little bit melancholic. See how difficult I've become!

By late August Mary had all her travel arrangements finalised and wrote to her colleagues in Perpignan:

> At last I can announce my return to the Midi. My trip was delayed by a fortnight because of difficulties obtaining a travel pass, but everything has been sorted out since yesterday and I'm leaving Paris on Tuesday evening 24 August on the express to Cerbère.

> At one point I had thought of spending a few hours in Toulouse between trains to see you all. Eventually I decided to continue my journey to my destination. The train is direct and I have quite a lot of baggage with me and I think it would be wiser to avoid the two changes which I would have otherwise had to make. I would love to see you and if it doesn't disturb you too much I'm thinking of going to Toulouse for the weekend of September 4–5.

In her book *Over the Highest Mountains*, Alice Resch, a Norwegian who worked with Helga Holbek in the Quakers' Toulouse office, described Mary's appearance when she visited her colleagues shortly after her release from Fresnes: "She arrived in our office, as attractive and well groomed as always, as if she just made a journey like any other. What a party we had!"

In Prades, Mary's friend Pablo Casals was overjoyed at the news of her release and excitedly wrote on August 3:

> Dear Miss Elmes, Eureka! What a pleasure to see you again. I will be going to Perpignan early in September … I hope to find you've come back to life after your recent exhaustions.
>
> The good that you have done has been crowned and you have a right to be proud of it.

Upon her release Mary was advised that she was entitled to the salary that had accrued during her time in prison. In a typical gesture of selflessness she refused to take the full amount due and returned the bulk of the money so that it could be used to help those more needy than herself. On 23 September, Eleanor Cohu of the Marseille office wrote to her:

> I learned also that you made a gift of Fr.5,000 to Secours Quakers, not wishing to retain all of your salary. This, my dear Mary, I am sorry to learn, although I appreciate the generosity which prompted you to do this. I really believe that the other Friends would have infinitely preferred you to retain the sum in full for

> yourself, as a small indemnity for the distressing experience you have had to undergo.
>
> I hope you will succeed in getting away at last for a real rest and good feed, and I am looking forward to seeing you soon again.

Since Mary never kept a diary she left no record of her prison experience. Although she dismissed her time as a prisoner with the observation that "we all suffered inconveniences at that time", her son and daughter believe that it marked her for the rest of her life. Certainly, the move from Toulouse prison to Fresnes on 31 March must have greatly alarmed her. From then on she would be in the hands of the Gestapo, who had turned the basement of the prison into a torture chamber. Despite her own precarious situation she still felt pity for the German soldier escorting her to Paris on the train: "… the poor man … many of those Germans weren't at all inclined to be soldiers or to fight the French … they'd been torn away from their ordinary life and made into soldiers and they didn't want to be", she later told interviewer John Baskin.

A sensation of what life was like in Fresnes and the casual barbarity that prevailed there emerges from the pages of the diary of Agnes Humbert, a *résistante* who was held in the prison the year before Mary before being deported to a forced labour camp. Agnes' entry for 20 January 1942 makes for stark reading:

> The days go by, dismal, dark and freezing cold …. Yesterday I heard the screams of a man being tortured. When the screams died down, they were followed by deep, throaty laughter. I don't know which was the more terrible. The laughter, I think.

At Fresnes conditions were no better than the military prison in Toulouse: "It was cold … we were very cramped. Three people in a cell that was for one person, with the window nailed up. … You mustn't look outside … there was light but no air." For a toilet the prisoners shared a bucket. A shower was provided once a fortnight. The only exercise available to the prisoners was walking around a small square courtyard, "a little surrounded place which was supervised by the soldiers who walked along a sort of elevated place".

For several weeks one of Mary's cellmates was a fifty-year-old Corsican *résistante* named Faustine Chiarelli. The two women became friends and helped to distract each other from the brutal reality of life in Fresnes until one day when Faustine was abruptly deported to work as a slave labourer in Germany. The threat of deportation was a constant fear among the prisoners in Fresnes and all lived in dread of a sudden summons to gather their belongings and prepare to leave. "The only danger that I ran was that they'd put me on a train and send me off", Mary recalled, "as they did with other people … not just the Jews, anybody … one knew it might happen, one sensed that it might happen but you didn't think about it all the time, luckily."

Asked how she passed the time in prison, Mary replied:

> That was the terrible thing … well the Quakers sent me books … so I had something to read … there was a sort of library that circulated and you could have a book. … But they sent me personally books, which kept me going … and then of course we talked, amongst ourselves … it was quite interesting. I met very interesting and strange people … some people were a lot more miserable than me.

After Faustine's departure Mary must have thought she had seen the last of her cellmate and friend, but miraculously the Corsican survived and was liberated by the Red Cross at the end of the war. When the two women renewed their friendship Mary invited Faustine to become godmother of her first child, Caroline. Sadly, Faustine's experience during her time in the east had left her a physically broken woman. She died when her goddaughter was eight years old.

Mary also remembered another of the prisoners who passed through her cell:

> She was a young Polish woman … that had been arrested and separated from her little two-year-old child …. I was liberated

> while she was still there but she never knew what had happened to her child .... I don't know [why she was arrested] ... people didn't discuss why, you see, because you mustn't talk too much about yourself and let your suspicions grow .... She was very nice, she was younger than me .... I was 35. I had my thirty-fifth birthday in Fresnes ... there was no celebration."

Whatever effects moves by the AFSC, the Red Cross and sundry diplomats had on securing Mary's release from Fresnes, she herself reserved most of the credit for her mother:

> It was thanks to my mother that I was really released ... because I was a neutral, Ireland was neutral at that time ... when she heard that I'd been arrested like that, quite a long time after, because she was ill and I didn't want her to know about it but she found out anyway and she approached the senator who represented Trinity [College Dublin], whose name was Kingsley Moore, and he made representations to the ... German Embassy [in Dublin] and that's how I got out. ... It was thanks to my mother and her intervention.

8

A Light in the Darkness

After their narrow escape from the Gestapo in Toulouse, Réné and Mario, fretting over their separation from their parents, arrived at the presbytery in Marssac exhausted and starving. There they joined five other boys who were also in hiding. After a few days of rest, food and cossetting by their hosts, the boys had recovered their strength. At this point they were taken into the homes of two separate local families, helped by a M. Pic, a friend of their father's. Réné was fostered by M. Pic's sister, Marguerite Raufaste, who lived nearby in Albi. She and her husband became his foster parents; their daughter, Josette, assumed the role of his godmother. In time the family grew so fond of young Réné that at one point Marguerite hoped to adopt him.

Marguerite's connection with the Freunds went back some years. At the time of their attempted escape from France, Marguerite, who already knew the family, had been staying at the same hotel on the Franco-Swiss border. The brothers' father had left instructions that they were to be baptised as Catholics. This request was duly carried out on 17 December 1942 when Father Bézard performed the ceremony in the village church. By now the boys had been enrolled in the local Catholic school. In his account of his and André's rescue of Réné and Mario, Father Bézard described how the children's mother, Eva, came to live in Marssac in May 1943 following her release from Gurs camp and rented an apartment in the village. The family remained in Marssac until the end of the war, when they moved to England, where Eva had a brother. Once there the family again benefitted from the generosity of the Quakers, who took on responsibility for the brothers' education.

In 1958 Réné made the trip back to Marssac to renew his links with the village and personally thank those whose courage and kindness had helped save the lives of he and his brother. Their studies in England complete, Réné and Mario – by now known respectively as Ron Friend and Michael Freund – emigrated to Canada. Michael pursued a career similar to his late father's, specialising in industrial engineering, while Ron left Canada for the United States in 1969, where he was tenured as professor of psychology at Stonybrook University in New York until he retired in 2003. Ron married and had a son; Michael had two daughters. As Ron recalls:

> My mother was allowed into England in 1947 where she stayed with her younger brother, our uncle Max Brauer, who was married to our aunt 'Bunty', who was a Quaker. My mother worked as a house-keeper in Lancashire and then as a cook in a prep school named Boarzell, in Sussex, where I was briefly a student, until about 1950.

Ron's mother later emigrated to Montevideo to be with a school friend before returning in the 1950s to Frankfurt, where she had another brother. In the late 1990s she moved to Canada to live with Michael.

Ron's visit to Marssac in 1957 had brought him back into direct touch with Father Bézard, who helped fill in the background to his escape from the safe house in Toulouse in that deadly summer of 1942. Yet, at the back of his mind a nagging question lingered: who had taken him out of Rivesaltes in the first place? It would entail a wait of almost seventy years before Ron found the answer to his question and finally discovered the name of his saviour.

***

Following her release from Fresnes Prison, Mary went back to work after her short holiday. The final transport might have rumbled out of Rivesaltes but the deportations from France were an ongoing reality and would continue to be so right up to the days preceding the Liberation of

Paris in August 1944. Those Jews still in hiding needed help to escape. Throughout the war a network of escape lines had been set up by people sympathetic to the plight of those fleeing France for their lives. Escaped prisoners of war, downed Allied airmen and fugitive Jews all benefitted from these routes of safety. A Lithuanian-born French Jewish engineer named George Garel created the eponymous Garel Line – which had links with the OSE – helping Jews and others to escape from France into Switzerland and providing false identity papers and visas. It remains unclear whether Mary ever worked directly with these individuals, although she did have contact in the camps and elsewhere with the OSE and other relief agencies whose trust she had earned and who were actively involved in this type of activity. Her incarceration by the Gestapo for six months would also suggest that she was regarded by the authorities as a significant player in helping Jews escape from France.

From the time of her release until the liberation of the Pyrenees-Orientales in April 1944 Mary went about her work knowing that she under constant surveillance by the French intelligence services, who belatedly came to the conclusion after the war that she was a person 'of morality'. She was also actively involved in maintaining the feeding progammes for patients in St Louis Hospital and for the local French population, especially children.

In 1946 Mary married Roger Danjou and the couple set up home together in Perpignan. Their first child, Caroline, was born in October 1946. A son, Patrick, followed in July 1948. Of her childhood, Caroline recalls:

> When we were young children, it wasn't something we talked about a lot. It wasn't something that was spoken about often because my father didn't want to hear anything more about the war. Because that was also a period that was very hard for her as well. She was in prison, and these were memories she didn't want to remember too much.
>
> When she arrived in Spain, she was very young … I think all that left a terrible mark on her. In addition, she had enormous responsibilities because she was in charge of the children's

> hospital. She had to be very organised. Obviously this must have influenced her personality.

For Patrick, although mindful of his mother's achievements, Mary was his mother first and foremost:

> She was very well educated, very intelligent … she knew a lot of things and was very determined. It's that especially, her determination … when you're a child you learn things little by little, without even realising that you're picking them up. There are conversations, somebody comes to the house, there are photographs. I had photographs in the drawer in my bedroom so from time to time I'd look at the photographs and ask 'what was that?' It was little by little, it's not like one day somebody said, 'I'll tell you my story'. Little by little we discovered the story of Spain and the hospitals. She'd tell us about an episode, she tell us for example about moving out of the hospital in Alicante … lorries …. But all that came in little snippets, it wasn't structured and regretfully she never wrote anything about it.

In 2003 Ron Friend retired from Stonybrook University and with his wife, Suzanne, and son, Patrick, relocated to Portland, Oregon. Now with extra time on his hands he could devote more effort to unravelling the mystery of his liberation from the camp of Rivesaltes where so many less fortunate than he and his brother languished in agony before being transported to their deaths. It was not until 2011, however, that his efforts would bear fruit in the form of an email from the OSE. Finally, Ron had a name: Mary Elmes. But where to find more information on this woman to whom he and so many others owed their lives?

The first clue lay in a compelling book called *Love and War in the Pyrenees*, written by British author Rosemary Bailey, which, for the first time, mentioned Mary Elmes and her work in the camps. Around this time the book had come to the attention of a Quaker and retired college lecturer named Bernard Wilson, who, with his wife, Janet, divides his time behind Britain and southwest France, where Rosemary's book is set. Coincidentally, I had also spotted the book and had picked up on the reference to Mary Elmes. Ron, Bernard and myself – at that point all strangers – were about to set off on the trail of this remarkable Irishwoman.

It would take some time but eventually Bernard and Ron's meticulous research culminated in 2013 with Mary being honoured as Righteous Among the Nations, Israel's highest honour for non-Jews who risked their own lives to save Jews during the Holocaust, the most famous recipient being Oskar Schindler. Bernard's attention had also been caught by a book called *Over the Highest Mountains* by Alice Resch, a Norwegian woman who worked with the Quaker delegation in Toulouse. As he explained:

> I was amazed to learn of the extent and impact of Quaker activity during that period. I knew that the Toulouse Quakers of today had only been in existence for a few years, and I wondered what they knew of what had happened in Toulouse seventy years before. The answer was – very little! But I was [encouraged] to write reviews for these two books and publish them on the Toulouse Quaker blog. To my surprise I began to receive messages from people who had read the blog and wanted to know more.

One of those who contacted Bernard through the blog was Ron. It was the beginning of a quest that would finally provide the missing link to a question that had perplexed him for most of his life. Bernard continued.

> Eventually we discovered the American Friends Service Committee and their vast archive. After spending several days poring over computers in the Mémorial [de la Shoah] in Paris I managed to persuade the AFSC activist in Philadelphia [Donald Davis] to send me six DVDs, containing the records relating to humanitarian work in France 1933 to 1950. Together, Ron and I began the task of finding the evidence we needed which would lead eventually to Mary Elmes being awarded the honour of

Righteous Gentile by Yad Vashem, the first Irish person to be so recognised.

Yad Vashem, Israel's official memorial to victims of the Holocaust, was founded in 1953 by the Israeli Parliament, the Knesset. Ten years later a commission headed by a retired justice of the country's Supreme Court was established to award the honorary title Righteous Among the Nations to suitable candidates, after scrupulously examining all the details of each case. On 12 March 2012 Ron submitted his testimony on Mary to Yad Vashem. Just over a year later all his efforts on her behalf bore fruit when she was honoured with the title. Sadly, Mary, who died in 2002, never received the award personally. On 27 June 2014 her son, daughter and great-grandchildren accepted, on her behalf, the Righteous certificate and medal at a ceremony near her former home in Perpignan. Earlier that same day – at a ceremony attended by local politicians and representatives of the French military and the Jewish community – a memorial stele was unveiled in her memory near the site of the children's colony at Canet-la-Plage, where Mary had worked with Lois Gunden to hide endangered children.

Commenting on Mary's belated recognition, Marc Masurovsky, co-founder of the Washington-based Holocaust Art Restitution Project and an archivist with the United States Holocaust Memorial Museum, noted:

> She should've just been recognised a lot earlier. It's too bad it took so long. People like Mary were godsends ... I'm sure there are hundreds, if not thousands, of people who are in her trust .... Even those who went to the camps, at least they did have that glimmer of hope when she was there. For the children who survived, well they owe it to her.

In an emotional speech at the Righteous ceremony in France, Ron thanked Mary for his life and the life of his son. In an interview, his brother, Michael, who was unable to attend the ceremony, echoed Ron's sentiments:

> I realise that I owe my life to her, my brother and I. I've often taken part in the [Holocaust] Remembrance Day ceremonies in Canada. I used to have a small private plane and I'd be flying in formation on Remembrance Day. I would certainly think of Mary Elmes on those occasions. I personally feel very grateful to Mary Elmes and I think that I'm just one of many who she saved.

Unfortunately, the true number of people who were rescued by Mary remains a mystery since the very nature of her work saving children made it impossible – and unsafe – to keep accurate records. Many of those she saved never knew the identity of the woman who had organised their escape and so could do nothing to highlight her efforts. One clue to the scale of her activities can be found in the explanatory panel that stands beside the stele unveiled in her name at Canet-la-Plage, which states:

> Here in front of you stood the 'Villa Saint-Christophe' which, from April 1941 to November 1942, housed a convalescent home for children from the internment camps.
>
> The institution was headed by Helen Penner and Lois Gunden, American Mennonites, helped by Mary Elmes [who was] in charge of the Quaker humanitarian section in Perpignan. Over three hundred children from the camp at Rivesaltes – Spaniards, as well as French, Polish, German and Austrian Jews – were cared for, and for certain of them, saved from deportation to the Nazi extermination camps ....

Coincidentally, Lois and Mary were named Righteous in the same year, 2013: Mary on 21 January, Lois on 27 February. Mary's award ceremony took place in 2014.

In 1946, the year her daughter was born, Mary retired from Secours Quakers. When the organisation closed its offices in Perpignan the following year she was guest of honour at the delegation's farewell dinner, which was attended by the local mayor and other officials who wished to express their gratitude to the Quakers for their relief efforts during the war. That same year the Quakers, represented by the Friends Service Council in London and the AFSC in the United States, were jointly awarded the Noble Peace Prize in recognition of their decades of humanitarian work.

After the Liberation of France in 1944, Rivesaltes served for four years as a prisoner-of-war camp holding German troops. At the end of the French–Algerian war in 1962 the camp took on yet another role, housing more than 20,000 'harkis' – Algerians who fought on the French side and had fled to France to avoid reprisals. Rivesaltes finally closed in 1965. Just over half a century later, in October 2015, Prime Minister Manuel Valls, himself a descendent of Catalan immigrants, officially inaugurated the memorial museum to the camp that now stands on the former site of Îlot F. The memorial is constructed in the form of giant slab of ochre cement that seems to emerge from the long trench it lies in, rising at a gentle slope as if metaphorically struggling to free itself from the soil that surrounds it. Once inside the visitor descends into a windowless building housing exhibits, photographs and video displays. The centre also includes an auditorium and teaching areas. At its official opening Prime Minister Valls declared that the memorial would say "loud and clear what for too long was whispered" – a reference to France's reluctance for decades to accept responsibility for the actions of its officials during the dark days of its recent history. In July 2017, speaking at the annual commemoration of *Opération Vent Printanier* near the site of the Vel d'Hiver stadium, French President Emmanuel Macron insisted that "it was indeed France that organised this [round-up] ... not a single German took part. ... It is convenient to see the Vichy Regime as born of nothingness, returned to nothingness. We cannot build pride upon a lie." It was not until 1995 that a French President acknowledged for the first time the state's role in the round-ups, when Jacques Chirac admitted that "France, the home of the Enlightenment and the Rights of Man, a land of welcome and asylum, on that day committed the irreparable."

Yet if there were many who were prepared to collaborate with the Nazis, others emerged willing to do all in their power to thwart their evil efforts. Paying tribute to one of those who never flinched, journalist and writer Joel Mettay had this to say:

> Darkness and fog. That's exactly what the Nazis were hoping for. Night and fog, which meant that nobody would see what they were doing. The Jewish people were going to disappear from the face of the planet without anyone realising and without anyone reacting. People like Mary Elmes, by their actions, they shone a light on this tragedy, this crime. So people could no longer say: 'I didn't know what was happening'. Because others illuminated what was being done in the darkness.

Speaking to the author shortly before this book was published, Ron Friend reflected on the woman who had saved the lives of he and his brother:

> Mary Elmes was a woman of extraordinary moral strength, courage and character. These personal qualities, combined with her exceptional language and organizational skills, were of maximum advantage when needed most in Franco's Spain and Vichy France. The Quakers were fortunate to have her lead their organization in Perpignan. The Spanish, Roma and Jewish internees in Camp de Rivesaltes were even more fortunate to receive the attention and aid she provided on a daily basis. I was a mere two-and-a-half years old when Mary Elmes took me out of the camp as the cattle wagons were regularly being loaded for Drancy and extermination with men, women and children – some even younger than me. It is now 75 years ago this month on September 26 [2017] that she drove my brother and I out of the Camp de Rivesaltes. I would not be writing these words if it was not for Mary Elmes.

Mary Elmes, Righteous Among the Nations
May 1908 – March 2002

References

Chapter 1

Quotes by Miguel Escalona Quesada are taken from Linda Palfreeman's book *Aristocrats, Adventurers and Ambulances.*

Queipo de Llano's quotes used in this chapter were cited by Linda Palfreeman in her book *Aristocrats, Adventurers and Ambulances* and originally appeared in Paul Preston's *The Spanish Holocaust.* I have also quoted from Linda Palfreeman's translations of firsthand testimonies of survivors of the exodus from Malaga to Almeria, which were used in the above book.

Quotes by Mary Elmes are from an interview conducted by American journalist John Baskin when she was in her eighties.

The *Manchester Guardian* report was published in early February 1937.

I have also drawn on Mark Derby's book *Petals and Bullets* for letters written by Dorothy Morris and her colleagues.

Mary's quote about the futility of war comes from an interview she did with Mexican filmmaker Marcela Arteaga in the 1990s, as does her reference to the orphan 'Tato'.

Letters written by Mary are from the Danjou family's private collection.

Letters written by members of the ambulance unit are from the British Quaker archives, Friends House, London, as is the Quaker fund-raising pamphlet.

Chapter 2

Edith Pye's report is from the archives of the AFSC, Philadelphia.

Gustav Regler's account was quoted by historian Paul Preston in his book *The Spanish Civil War.* It was originally published in Regler's book *The Owl of Minerva.*

Robert Capa's account of his visit to the camps comes from *Robert Capa: A Biography* by Richard Whelan.

Pablo Casals' account of his visit to the refugee camps on the beaches is taken from his book *Joy and Sorrows.*

Howard Kershner's report for the International Commission, as is the case with the other reports quoted in this chapter, form part of the AFSC archives in Philadelphia.

Mary's quote on the end of the Spanish Civil War is from journalist John Baskin's interview with her, while the one about her work reuniting families in the French camps is from an interview with Mexican filmmaker Marcela Arteaga.

Letters written by Mary to colleagues and officials are all from the AFSC files while those written to personal contacts come from the Danjou family collection.

Letters written by Dorothy Morris are again taken from Mark Derby's book *Petals and Bullets.*

Chapter 3

The report by Virginia Cowles, originally published in the *Sunday Times* on 16 June 1940, was reproduced in the same newspaper on 14 June 2014, under the headline 'Paris Falls Silent as Thousands Flee Nazis'.

The Daphne Wall quote is from her book *The World I Lost.*

Efraim Zuroff's quotes are taken from an interview by Andrew Gallimore, director of the Midas Productions documentary *It Tolls for Thee.*

Chapter 4

Letters and reports quoted in this chapter are from the AFSC files in Philadelphia.

The quotes from Joel Mettay are taken from his book *L'Archipel du Mépris.*

George Koltein was interviewed by the author for the Midas Productions documentary *It Tolls for Thee.*

Friedel Bohny-Reiter's diary was published as *Journal de Rivesaltes 1941–1942* in 1993.

Chapter 5

The Guardian report from the Vel d'Hiv was published as 'From Our Special Correspondent, Paris' on 3 September 1942.

George Koltein was interviewed by the author for the Midas Productions documentary *It Tolls for Thee.*

Ross McClelland's report of his meeting with Pétain and Laval, and his account of the deportation of foreign Jews from France in 1942, is from the United States Holocaust Memorial Museum Collection, gifted to them by his son, Kirk McClelland.

The letters from Mary come from the AFSC files.

Chapter 6

Ross McClelland's report of his meeting with Pétain and Laval, and his account of the deportation of foreign Jews from France in 1942, is from the United States Holocaust Memorial Museum Collection, gifted to them by his son, Kirk McClelland.

The quote from Joel Mettay comes from his book *L'Archipel Du Mépris*, while that from Alexandre Doulut comes from his book *Les Juifs au Camp de Rivesaltes.*

Reports and correspondence contained in this chapter are held in the AFSC archives.

Letters written by Mary to colleagues and officials are all from AFSC files while those written to personal contacts, e.g. Rose Duroux, come from the Danjou family collection.

Burritt Hiatt's journal quotations were supplied by journalist John Baskin.

The quote from Alice Resch comes from her memoir, *Over the Highest Mountains.*

The letter from Léa Drommelschlager to her infant son was quoted by Joel Mettay in *L'Archipel du Mépris*, originally quoted in Serge Klarsfeld's *Le Calendrier de la Persécution des Juifs en France: 1940–1944* (Éditions de la FFDIJF, 1993).

Interviews with Ron Friend (Réné Freund) and Michael (Mario) Freund were conducted for Midas Productions' documentary *It Tolls for Thee.*

Fr Bézard's account of the rescue of Réné and Mario Freund comes from a letter he wrote to Ron Friend (formerly Réné Freund) in 1958, who provided it to the author.

Friedel Bohny-Reiter's diary was published as *Journal de Rivesaltes 1941–1942* in 1993.

The quotes from Denis Peschanski come from his book *La France des Camps.*

John Baskin's quote on the true nature of the deportations comes from an interview with the producers of the documentary *It Tolls for Thee.*

Efraim Zuroff's quotes are taken from an interview with Andrew Gallimore, director of the Midas Productions documentary *It Tolls for Thee.*

The quote from Andrée Salomon of the OSE comes from Katy Hazan and George Weill's book, *Andrée Salomon: Une Femme de Lumiere.*

Chapter 7

Mary's quotes are taken from her interview with American journalist John Baskin.

AFSC correspondence referred to in this chapter is held in that organisation's archive, letters written by the Irish diplomats are stored in the archives of the Irish Department of Foreign Affairs while copies of letters written by Mary and her mother form part of the Danjou family collection.

The letter from Pablo Casals is part of the Danjou family collection.

Agnes Humbert's book on her time as a prisoner is entitled *Résistance.*

Chapter 8

The interviews quoted in this chapter were conducted for Midas Productions' documentary *It Tolls for Thee.*

Select Bibliography

The background to the events that framed Mary Elmes' humanitarian work in Spain and France have been have widely documented elsewhere. The following is a list of those publications that have directly enhanced my attempts to shed more light on this extraordinary woman and her achievements.

Rosemary Bailey, *Love and War in the Pyrenees*, London: Weidenfeld and Nicolson, 2008.

Roger Barrié, *Mémento Chronologique du Camp de Rivesaltes*, Pyrenées-Orientales: Musée Mémorial du Camp de Rivesaltes and Conseil Général des Pyrenées-Orientales, 2010.

Anthony Beaver, *The Battle for Spain: The Spanish Civil War 1936–1939*, London: Weidenfeld and Nicolson, 2006.

Christian Bernadac, *The 186 Steps*, Geneva: Ferni, 1978.

Friedel Bohny-Reiter, *Journal de Rivesaltes 1941–1942*, Geneva: Éditions Zoé, 1993.

Pablo Casals, *Joy and Sorrows: Reflections by Pablo Casals*, New York, NY: Simon and Schuster, 1970.

Virginia Cowles, 'Paris Falls Silent as Thousands Flee Nazis', *Sunday Times*, 16 June 1940 [reprinted 14 June 2014].

Mark Derby, *Petals and Bullets: Dorothy Morris – New Zealand Nurse in the Spanish Civil War*, Eastbourne: Sussex Academic Press, 2015.

Hannah Diamond, *Fleeing Hitler: France 1940*, Oxford University Press, 2007.

Alexandre Doulot, *Les Juifs au Camp de Rivesaltes: Internement et Deportation*, Paris: Mémorial du Camp de Rivesaltes and Lienart Éditons, 2014.

Guardian, The, 'From Our Special Correspondent, Paris', 3 September 1942.

Katy Hazan and George Weil, *Andrée Salomon: Une Femme de Lumiere*, Paris: Éditions Le Manuscrit, 2011.

Agnes Humbert, *Résistance: Memoirs of Occupied France* (translated by Barbara Mellor), London: Bloomsbury Publishing, 2004.

Arthur Koestler, *Spanish Testament*, London: Gollancz, 1937.

Arthur Koestler, *Scum of the Earth*, London: Jonathan Cape, 1941.

Joel Mettay, *L'Archipel Du Mépris: Histoire du Camp de Rivesaltes*; Canet: Éditions Trabucaire, 2008.

Linda Palfreeman, *Aristocrats, Adventurers and Ambulances: British Medical Units in the Spanish Civil War*, Eastbourne: Sussex Academic Press, 2014.

Denis Peschanski, *La France des Camps: L'Internement, 1938–1946*, Paris: Gallimard, 2002.

Rénée Poznanski, Denis Peschanski and Benoit Pouvreau, *Drancy: Un Camp en France*, Paris: Fayard, 2015.

Paul Preston, *The Spanish Holocaust: Inquisition and Extermination in Twentieth-Century Spain*, London: Harper Press, 2012.

Paul Preston, *The Spanish Civil War: Reaction, Revolution and Revenge*, London: Harper Perennial, 2016.

Anindya Raychaudhuri, *The Spanish Civil War: Exhuming a Buried Past*, Cardiff: University of Wales Press, 2013.

Gustav Regler, *The Owl of Minerva*, London: Rupert Hart-Davis, 1959.

Alice Resch Synnestvedt, *Over the Highest Mountains: A Memoir of Unexpected Heroism in France During World War II*, Pasadena, CA: International Productions, 2005.

Vivette Samuel, *Rescuing the Children: A Holocaust Memoir*, Madison, WI: University of Wisconsin Press, 2002.

Daphne Wall, *The World I Lost: A Memoir of Peace and War*, Rottingdean: Sortium, 2014.

Richard Whelan, *Robert Capa: A Biography*, Lincoln, NE: University of Nebraska Press, 1994.

Bernard S. Wilson, *See You Soon Caroline!*, King's Lynn: Shore Books and Design, 2014.

Howard Wriggins, *Picking Up the Pieces from Portugal to Palestine: Quaker Refuge Relief in World War II*, Lanham, MD: University Press of America, 2004.